OFFICIAL S
PAST
PAPERS
WITH ANSWERS

£1.99

W43

14 D

HIGHER

BIOLOGY
2009-2013

SQA

HODDER
GIBSON
LEARN MORE

Hodder Gibson is grateful to the copyright holders, as credited on the final page of the Question Section, for permission to use their material. Every effort has been made to trace the copyright holders and to obtain their permission for the use of copyright material. Hodder Gibson will be happy to receive information allowing us to rectify any error or omission in future editions.

Hachette UK's policy is to use papers that are natural, renewable and recyclable products and made from wood grown in sustainable forests. The logging and manufacturing processes are expected to conform to the environmental regulations of the country of origin.

Orders: please contact Bookpoint Ltd, 130 Park Drive, Abingdon, Oxon OX14 4SE. Telephone: (44) 01235 827720. Fax: (44) 01235 400454.

Lines are open 9.00–5.00, Monday to Saturday, with a 24-hour message answering service. Visit our website at www.hoddereducation.co.uk. Hodder Gibson can be contacted direct on: Tel: 0141 848 1609; Fax: 0141 889 6315; email: hoddergibson@hodder.co.uk

This collection first published in 2013 by

Hodder Gibson, an imprint of Hodder Education,

An Hachette UK Company

2a Christie Street

Paisley PA1 1NB

BrightRED
PUBLISHING

Hodder Gibson is grateful to Bright Red Publishing Ltd for collaborative work in preparation of this book and all SQA Past Paper and National 5 Model Paper titles 2013.

Typeset by PDQ Digital Media Solutions Ltd, Bungay, Suffolk NR35 1BY

Printed in the UK

A catalogue record for this title is available from the British Library

ISBN 978-1-4718-0271-3

3 2 1

2014 2013

Introduction

Study Skills – what you need to know to pass exams!

Pause for thought

Many students might skip quickly through a page like this. After all, we all know how to revise. Do you really though?

Think about this:

"IF YOU ALWAYS DO WHAT YOU ALWAYS DO, YOU WILL ALWAYS GET WHAT YOU HAVE ALWAYS GOT."

Do you like the grades you get? Do you want to do better? If you get full marks in your assessment, then that's great! Change nothing! This section is just to help you get that little bit better than you already are.

There are two main parts to the advice on offer here. The first part highlights fairly obvious things but which are also very important. The second part makes suggestions about revision that you might not have thought about but which WILL help you.

Part 1

DOH! It's so obvious but …

Start revising in good time

Don't leave it until the last minute – this will make you panic.

Make a revision timetable that sets out work time AND play time.

Sleep and eat!

Obvious really, and very helpful. Avoid arguments or stressful things too – even games that wind you up. You need to be fit, awake and focused!

Know your place!

Make sure you know exactly **WHEN and WHERE** your exams are.

Know your enemy!

Make sure you know what to expect in the exam.

How is the paper structured?

How much time is there for each question?

What types of question are involved?

Which topics seem to come up time and time again?

Which topics are your strongest and which are your weakest?

Are all topics compulsory or are there choices?

Learn by DOING!

There is no substitute for past papers and practice papers – they are simply essential! Tackling this collection of papers and answers is exactly the right thing to be doing as your exams approach.

Part 2

People learn in different ways. Some like low light, some bright. Some like early morning, some like evening / night. Some prefer warm, some prefer cold. But everyone uses their BRAIN and the brain works when it is active. Passive learning – sitting gazing at notes – is the most INEFFICIENT way to learn anything. Below you will find tips and ideas for making your revision more effective and maybe even more enjoyable. What follows gets your brain active, and active learning works!

Activity 1 – Stop and review

Step 1

When you have done no more than 5 minutes of revision reading STOP!

Step 2

Write a heading in your own words which sums up the topic you have been revising.

Step 3

Write a summary of what you have revised in no more than two sentences. Don't fool yourself by saying, 'I know it but I cannot put it into words'. That just means you don't know it well enough. If you cannot write your summary, revise that section again, knowing that you must write a summary at the end of it. Many of you will have notebooks full of blue/black ink writing. Many of the pages will not be especially attractive or memorable so try to liven them up a bit with colour as you are reviewing and rewriting. **This is a great memory aid, and memory is the most important thing.**

Activity 2 — Use technology!

Why should everything be written down? Have you thought about 'mental' maps, diagrams, cartoons and colour to help you learn? And rather than write down notes, why not record your revision material?

What about having a text message revision session with friends? Keep in touch with them to find out how and what they are revising and share ideas and questions.

Why not make a video diary where you tell the camera what you are doing, what you think you have learned and what you still have to do? No one has to see or hear it but the process of having to organise your thoughts in a formal way to explain something is a very important learning practice.

Be sure to make use of electronic files. You could begin to summarise your class notes. Your typing might be slow but it will get faster and the typed notes will be easier to read than the scribbles in your class notes. Try to add different fonts and colours to make your work stand out. You can easily Google relevant pictures, cartoons and diagrams which you can copy and paste to make your work more attractive and **MEMORABLE**.

Activity 3 – This is it. Do this and you will know lots!

Step 1

In this task you must be very honest with yourself! Find the SQA syllabus for your subject (www.sqa.org.uk). Look at how it is broken down into main topics called MANDATORY knowledge. That means stuff you MUST know.

Step 2

BEFORE you do ANY revision on this topic, write a list of everything that you already know about the subject. It might be quite a long list but you only need to write it once. It shows you all the information that is already in your long-term memory so you know what parts you do not need to revise!

Step 3

Pick a chapter or section from your book or revision notes. Choose a fairly large section or a whole chapter to get the most out of this activity.

With a buddy, use Skype, Facetime, Twitter or any other communication you have, to play the game "If this is the answer, what is the question?". For example, if you are revising Geography and the answer you provide is "meander", your buddy would have to make up a question like "What is the word that describes a feature river where it flows slowly and bends often from side?".

Make up 10 "answers" based on the content of the chapter or section you are using. Give this to your buddy to solve while you solve theirs.

Step 4

Construct a wordsearch of at least 10 X 10 squares. You can make it as big as you like but keep it realistic. Work together with a group of friends. Many apps allow you to make wordsearch puzzles online. The words and phrases can go in any direction and phrases can be split. Your puzzle must only contain facts linked to the topic you are revising. Your task is to find 10 bits of information to hide in your puzzle but you must not repeat information that you used in Step 3. DO NOT show where the words are. Fill up empty squares with random letters. Remember to keep a note of where your answers are hidden but do not show your friends. When you have a complete puzzle, exchange it with a friend to solve each other's puzzle.

Step 5

Now make up 10 questions (not "answers" this time) based on the same chapter used in the previous two tasks. Again, you must find NEW information that you have not yet used. Now it's getting hard to find that new information! Again, give your questions to a friend to answer.

Step 6

As you have been doing the puzzles, your brain has been actively searching for new information. Now write a NEW LIST that contains only the new information you have discovered when doing the puzzles. Your new list is the one to look at repeatedly for short bursts over the next few days. Try to remember more and more of it without looking at it. After a few days, you should be able to add words from your second list to your first list as you increase the information in your long-term memory.

FINALLY! Be inspired...

Make a list of different revision ideas and beside each one write **THINGS I HAVE** tried, **THINGS I WILL** try and **THINGS I MIGHT** try. Don't be scared of trying something new.

And remember – "FAIL TO PREPARE AND PREPARE TO FAIL!"

Higher Biology

The course

The Higher Biology Course is made up of three National Units. These are *Cell Biology, Genetics and Adaptation* and *Control and Regulation*. Each Unit has three outcomes which are assessed. These are Knowledge and Understanding, Problem Solving and Practical Abilities. You will be assessed in the outcomes for each Unit by your school or college on a pass or fail basis.

How the course is graded

To gain a Course award, you must pass the assessment for each Unit and take an examination set and marked by SQA. Your grade for the Course depends on your performance in the examination. Grades range from A to D. As a rough guide, to achieve grade A you will need to score 70% or more of the marks available for the examination, a B needs 60% and a C needs 50%. Grade D is awarded to candidates whose performance falls just a little short of 50%.

The exam

The examination is a single question paper with 130 marks, divided into three sections.

Section A contains 30 objective test items (multiple choice questions) for 30 marks.

Section B contains 80 short answer marks across about 14 or 15 questions. One of the questions always relates to an experiment or investigation and another is based on a set of data.

Section C has two extended response questions worth 10 marks each. Each Section C question has a choice of one from two. One of the questions in this section has a mark for coherence and another mark for relevance.

The question paper gives the Units equal weighting, with about 95 marks for Knowledge and Understanding and about 35 marks for Problem Solving overall. You will have 2 hours and 30 minutes to complete the paper.

This book contains five examples of examination question papers and their National standard answers to help you prepare for your own examination in Higher Biology.

Some hints and tips

In looking at thousands of candidates' papers each year, examiners often see good examination techniques but also common mistakes which are made year after year. This section should help you develop your exam technique and hopefully avoid common mistakes. It should also let you make the best use of the questions in this book and the all-important answers supplied with them.

Where candidates often get it right

Candidates get a lot of things right! The points below describe some of these areas – make sure you get them right too.

1   Section A contains 30 multiple choice questions. This section is usually done very well by candidates. The general points to remember in answering Section A are:

- Do not spend more than **30 minutes** on the section.
- Answer on a grid. Make sure the grid has your name pre-printed on it.
- **Do not leave blanks** – complete the grid for each question as you work through.

- Try to answer each question in your head **without** looking at the options. If your answer is there – you are home and dry!
- If you're not certain, choose the answer that seemed most attractive on **first** reading the answer options.
- If you are not sure, try to eliminate options before making your guess. If you can eliminate three you will be left with the correct answer even if you do not recognise it!

2   Overall, candidates' spelling is good, but watch for these words – you can lose marks by spelling them incorrectly, and many do!

- pituitary
- glycogen
- glucagon
- phospholipid
- phototropism.

3   Questions which combine ideas from different Units are tough. Many candidates obviously spend time on these and they learn the common linking questions. Make sure you have understood the following links:

- metabolic pathways such as glycolysis or the Calvin cycle linked to enzyme action
- energy release linked to active transport
- gene mutation linked to amino acid sequence errors in protein
- variation linked to natural selection.

4   Some candidates with generally weak papers write an almost unbelievably good extended response answer in Section C. They have presumably learned the area well in hope of the question appearing. Spotting questions is usually dangerous but it is a good idea to have answers to a few commonly asked extended response questions well learned.

5   We usually see very good graph drawing by candidates – what are they doing right?

- Putting in zeros to scales as appropriate.
- Using scales which extend beyond the highest and lowest values in data – if the highest value is 27, then the scale of the axis must extend to this and preferably beyond – say 30.
- Making sure that the scales are labelled directly from the headings in the data table and ensuring that units are included.
- In Higher Biology we look for straight lines connecting the points of a line graph – most candidates realise that this will require a ruler! A transparent ruler is the best!

6   Most candidates look at the past paper answers along with the questions – this is good practice. Here are examples in which careful wording makes the answer acceptable:

- In describing viral attack on cells, we need candidates to be clear which nucleic acid they are writing about and use the terms **viral** DNA/RNA and **host** DNA/RNA.
- In describing the effects of ADH on kidney tubules, we need candidates to be clear that ADH increases the permeability of kidney tubules **to water**.
- In describing what makes a species, we need candidates to be clear that they **interbreed** to produce **fertile** offspring.
- In describing differentiation of cells, we look for the idea of genes being switched on **or** off but not on and off.

7   Some candidates use a highlighter to remind themselves of important points they read within a question – this is very good practice.

8   We see lots of candidates getting marks for numerical answers – they clearly use their calculators effectively. Remember, most numerical answers are limited to numbers with a maximum of two decimal places.

9   We see very few blanks left in question papers, which is a great technique. Have a go using the words in the question – you never know!

10 Finally – candidates' handwriting is usually good. It is in their own interest that their handwriting is clearly legible – make sure yours is too!

Where candidates sometimes get it wrong

There are techniques and practices which some candidates clearly miss out on and certain mistakes are very commonly seen. The points below are hints on how to maximise the marks you score.

1   Make sure you finish the paper – spend a maximum of 30 minutes on Section A, about 90 minutes on Section B and leave about 30 minutes for Section C.

2   Use the language of the question in your answers if you can – it will help keep you on the right track.

3   Marks can be lost for failure to use the accepted biological language which is found in the Arrangements document – it is safer to use terms from there in your answers. You should have a copy of the Arrangements – it can be downloaded from the SQA website.

4   Check the mark allocation and support lines in each question you attempt – if there is more than one mark there will be more than one support line and you will need to make more than one point.

5   If a question asks you to **state**, **name** or **give** in a question, then it's likely that only a short answer is needed. On the other hand, if you are asked to **describe** or **explain** something, you will need a longer answer.

6   In some questions, the wording is crucial and often contains a piece of information which is vital in reaching the correct answer. This is very often the case in the data question – always read the question a couple of times.

7   There will be a few words printed in **bold**. Take careful note of these, because the bold word will be very important in finding your answer.

8   You will always be asked to draw a graph – make sure you choose scales to fill most of the graph paper and use a ruler to connect the points in a line graph.

9   When doing calculations use the space for calculation provided – you will probably need it, and markers look at working in case it deserves a mark, even if the final answer is wrong.

10 Avoid using words like **it** and **they** – make sure you say what **it** actually is or what **they** actually are.

11 There is always a practical question. Make sure you know what a variable is, why controls are needed and how reliability can be improved in an investigation. Take a few minutes to read the question and try to visualise what is actually happening – a scribbled drawing on your scrap paper can help.

12 Candidates sometimes try to draw conclusions when they are simply asked for a description of a graph. A description only uses values to describe the trends in the data but does not attempt to explain them in any way.

13 When describing a graph line, ensure that you quote data points and units. In comparing graphical investigation results, it is good practice to use comparative terms such as **lower** or **higher** rather than absolute terms such as **low** or **high**.

14 When describing changes in tabulated data, always quote values to make it clear where trends in the data change.

15 Many good candidates lose marks for the use of words such as **never** and **always** – it's better to consider if words such as **sometimes**, **usually** or **often** might be better. Don't be tempted to say that an adaptation can **stop** or **prevent** competition – it's better to say it **reduces** competition. Don't be tempted to say that corrective mechanisms **stop** skin sweating – it's better to say sweating is **reduced**.

16 There are several metabolic pathways which are important in Higher Biology. Make sure you are able to give the consequences of a blocked step in a metabolic pathway shown in a question.

17 Many candidates have trouble with chromosome numbers in cells. Most cells have the diploid chromosome number, meaning they have two sets of chromosomes, but gametes are usually haploid, with only one set. Be careful about quoting the human chromosome complement – not all organisms are human!

18 It is easy to lose marks when notating the symbols of sex linked alleles – remember the allele must be associated with the sex chromosome on which it's found using a super-script, for example, the genotype of a male with the sex-linked allele R would be notated as $X^R Y$.

19 If you run out of space for your answer, or want to make a change, ensure that you note down where you have put your changed answer, especially if it has had to go at the back of the booklet. Remember, there will always be a second graph grid at the back of the booklet if you need it. It's difficult to make changes to an incorrectly drawn graph – better score through and start again.

20 Section C is usually very challenging for candidates – 10 marks worth of extended writing is tough for anyone. Here are a few tips:

*   The two questions in Section C offer a choice – ensure that you give yourself a few minutes to make your choice. This is crucial because nearly every year one of the choices turns out to be a bit easier that the other. Note down the key words for each option – which seems more likely to yield marks?

*   Always write the title above your answer – it can sometimes contribute to your answer.

*   Diagrams are great for extended responses because they can be quicker than writing things out if you are short of time. Remember that diagrams must be labelled and, where there are arrows, the arrowheads must be clear and pointing in the right direction.

*   In Question 2, there is a mark for coherence and another for relevance – don't waste these! Coherence is about writing logically or in sections. The question title might suggest that there are two sections to the answer – make sure you separate your answer into the two parts and give each a short title. Relevance is really about not being irrelevant – if the question is about aerobic respiration, don't write anything about anaerobic!

Good luck!

Remember that the rewards for passing Higher Biology are well worth it! Your pass will help you get the future you want for yourself. In the exam, be confident in your own ability. If you're not sure how to answer a question, trust your instincts and just give it a go anyway. Keep calm and don't panic! GOOD LUCK!

HIGHER

2009

[BLANK PAGE]

FOR OFFICIAL USE

Total for
Sections
B and C

X007/301

NATIONAL
QUALIFICATIONS
2009

THURSDAY, 28 MAY
1.00 PM – 3.30 PM

BIOLOGY

HIGHER

Fill in these boxes and read what is printed below.

Full name of centre

Town

Forename(s)

Surname

Date of birth
  Day Month Year   Scottish candidate number   Number of seat

SECTION A–Questions 1—30 (30 marks)

Instructions for completion of Section A are given on page two.

For this section of the examination you must use an **HB pencil**.

SECTIONS B AND C (100 marks)

1   (a)   All questions should be attempted.

      (b)   It should be noted that in **Section C** questions 1 and 2 each contain a choice.

2   The questions may be answered in any order but all answers are to be written in the spaces provided in this answer book, **and must be written clearly and legibly in ink**.

3   Additional space for answers will be found at the end of the book. If further space is required, supplementary sheets may be obtained from the invigilator and should be inserted inside the **front** cover of this book.

4   The numbers of questions must be clearly inserted with any answers written in the additional space.

5   Rough work, if any should be necessary, should be written in this book and then scored through when the fair copy has been written. If further space is required a supplementary sheet for rough work may be obtained from the invigilator.

6   Before leaving the examination room you must give this book to the invigilator. If you do not, you may lose all the marks for this paper.

Read carefully

1 Check that the answer sheet provided is for **Biology Higher (Section A)**.

2 For this section of the examination you must use an **HB pencil**, and where necessary, an eraser.

3 Check that the answer sheet you have been given has **your name**, **date of birth**, **SCN** (Scottish Candidate Number) and **Centre Name** printed on it.

Do not change any of these details.

4 If any of this information is wrong, tell the Invigilator immediately.

5 If this information is correct, **print** your name and seat number in the boxes provided.

6 The answer to each question is **either** A, B, C or D. Decide what your answer is, then, using your pencil, put a horizontal line in the space provided (see sample question below).

7 There is **only one correct** answer to each question.

8 Any rough working should be done on the question paper or the rough working sheet, **not** on your answer sheet.

9 At the end of the exam, put the **answer sheet for Section A inside the front cover of this answer book**.

Sample Question

The apparatus used to determine the energy stored in a foodstuff is a

A calorimeter

B respirometer

C klinostat

D gas burette.

The correct answer is **A**—calorimeter. The answer **A** has been clearly marked in **pencil** with a horizontal line (see below).

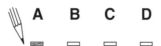

Changing an answer

If you decide to change your answer, carefully erase your first answer and using your pencil fill in the answer you want. The answer below has been changed to **D**.

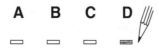

SECTION A

All questions in this section should be attempted.

Answers should be given on the separate answer sheet provided.

1. Which of the following is **not** surrounded by a membrane?

   A   Nucleus

   B   Ribosome

   C   Chloroplast

   D   Mitochondrion

2. The diagram below shows a plant cell which has been placed in a salt solution.

   Which line in the table describes correctly the salt solution and the state of the plant cell?

	Salt solution	State of cell
A	hypertonic	plasmolysed
B	hypertonic	turgid
C	hypotonic	flaccid
D	hypotonic	plasmolysed

3. Thin sections of beetroot and rhubarb tissue were immersed in the same sucrose solution for the same time. This resulted in the plasmolysis of 0% of the beetroot cells and 20% of the rhubarb cells.

   Which of the following statements can be deduced from these results?

   A   The sucrose solution was hypertonic to the beetroot cells.

   B   The sucrose solution was hypotonic to the rhubarb cells.

   C   The contents of the beetroot cells were hypotonic to the contents of the rhubarb cells.

   D   The contents of the rhubarb cells were hypotonic to the contents of the beetroot cells.

4. The total sunlight energy landing on an ecosystem is 4 million kilojoules per square metre (kJm^{-2}). Four percent of this is fixed during photosynthesis and five percent of this fixed energy is passed on to the primary consumers. What is the energy intake of the primary consumers?

   A $800\ kJm^{-2}$

   B $8000\ kJm^{-2}$

   C $20\ 000\ kJm^{-2}$

   D $360\ 000\ kJm^{-2}$

5. The diagram below shows a chromatogram of four plant pigments.

   The R_f value of each is calculated by dividing the furthest distance the pigment has moved, by the distance the solvent has moved from the origin.

   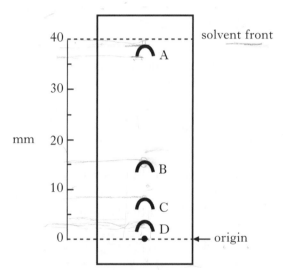

   Which pigment has an R_f value closest to 0·4?

6. The diagram below shows energy transfer within a cell.

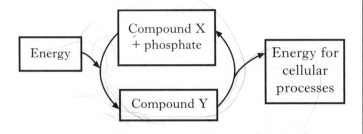

Which line in the table below identifies correctly compounds X and Y?

	X	Y
A	glucose	ATP
B	glucose	ADP
C	ADP	ATP
D	ATP	glucose

7. Which line in the table below shows correctly the sites of stages in aerobic respiration?

Citric acid   electron transport chain

	Glycolysis	Krebs Cycle	Cytochrome System
A	Cristae of Mitochondrion	Matrix of Mitochondrion	Cytoplasm
B	Cytoplasm	Cristae of Mitochondrion	Matrix of Mitochondrion
C	Cytoplasm	Matrix of Mitochondrion	Cristae of Mitochondrion
D	Matrix of Mitochondrion	Cytoplasm	Cristae of Mitochondrion

8. Which of the following is **not** composed of amino acids?

A Glucagon

B Collagen

C Amylase

D Cellulose

9. The table below refers to the mass of DNA in certain human body cells.

Cell type	Mass of DNA in cell $(\times 10^{-12}\,g)$
liver	6·6
lung	6·6
P	3·3
Q	0·0

Which of the following is most likely to identify correctly cell types P and Q?

	P	Q
A	kidney cell	sperm cell
B	sperm cell	mature red blood cell
C	mature red blood cell	sperm cell
D	nerve cell	mature red blood cell

10. Which line in the table below identifies correctly cellular defence mechanisms in plants which protect them against micro-organisms and herbivores?

	Defence against micro-organisms	Defence against herbivores
A	antibodies	resins
B	tannins	cyanide
C	spines	cyanide
D	resins	antibodies

11. In poultry, males have two X chromosomes and females have one X chromosome and one Y chromosome.

The gene for feather-barring is sex-linked.

The allele for barred feathers is dominant to the allele for non-barred feathers.

A non-barred male is crossed with a barred female.

What ratio of offspring would be expected?

A   1 barred male : 1 barred female

B   1 non-barred male : 1 non-barred female

C   1 barred male : 1 non-barred female

D   1 non-barred male : 1 barred female

12. The table below shows some genotypes and phenotypes associated with a form of anaemia.

Genotype	Phenotype
AA	Unaffected
AS	Sickle cell trait
SS	Acute sickle cell anaemia

A person with sickle cell trait and an unaffected person have a child together.

What are the chances of the child having acute sickle cell anaemia?

A   none

B   1 in 4

C   1 in 2

D   1 in 1

13. Which of the following statements refers to a gene mutation?

A   A change in the chromosome number caused by non-disjunction.

B   A change in the number of genes on a chromosome caused by duplication.

C   A change in the structure of a chromosome caused by translocation.

D   A change in the base sequence of DNA caused by substitution.

14. Polyploidy in plants may result from

A   total spindle failure during meiosis

B   hybridisation between varieties of the same species

C   homologous chromosomes binding at chiasmata

D   the failure of linked genes to separate.

15. Which of the following is an example of artificial selection?

A   Industrial melanism in moths

B   DDT resistance in mosquitoes

C   Increased milk yield in dairy cattle

D   Decreasing effect of antibiotics on bacteria

16. The diagram below shows stages involved in the genetic engineering of bacteria to produce human insulin.

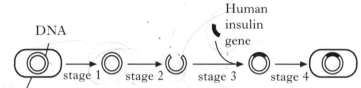

Which line in the table below shows the stages of this process in which endonuclease and ligase are involved?

	Stage involving endonuclease	Stage involving ligase
A	2	4
B	2	3
C	3	2
D	4	3

[Turn over

17. The statements below describe methods of maintaining a water balance in fish.

1 Salts actively absorbed by chloride secretory cells

2 Salts actively secreted by chloride secretory cells

3 Low rate of kidney filtration

4 High rate of kidney filtration

Which of these are used by **freshwater** bony fish?

A 1 and 3 only

B 2 and 4 only

C 1 and 4 only

D 2 and 3 only

18. The graph below shows the net energy gain or loss from hunting and eating prey of different masses.

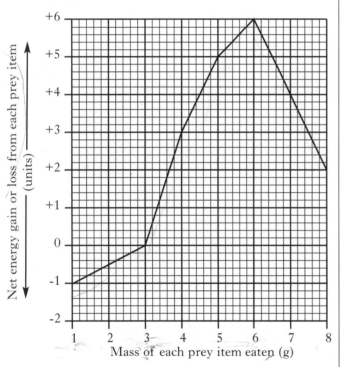

It can be concluded from the graph that

A prey between 1 g and 3 g are rarer than prey between 3 g and 6 g

B hunting and eating prey above 6 g involves a net energy loss

C prey of 8 g contain less energy than prey of mass 6 g

D hunting and eating prey below 3 g involves a net energy loss.

19. Which of the following statements about habituation is correct?

A It is a temporary change in behaviour.

B It occurs only in young animals.

C It is a social mechanism for defence.

D It is a permanent change in behaviour.

20. Some animal species live in social groups for defence.

Which of the following statements describes a change which could result from an increase in the size of such a social group?

A Individuals are able to spend less time feeding.

B There are fewer times when more than one animal is looking for predators.

C Each animal can spend more time looking for predators than foraging.

D Individuals are able to spend less time looking for predators.

21. Phenylketonuria is a condition that results from

A differential gene expression

B chromosome non-disjunction

C a vitamin deficiency

D an inherited gene mutation.

22. The plant growth substance indole acetic acid (IAA) is of benefit to humans because it can function

A as a herbicide and to break dormancy

B as a herbicide and as a rooting powder

C in the germination of barley and to break dormancy

D as a rooting powder and in the germination of barley.

23. The graph below shows changes in the α-amylase concentration and starch content of a barley grain during early growth and development.

- - - - - - starch content

————— α-amylase concentration

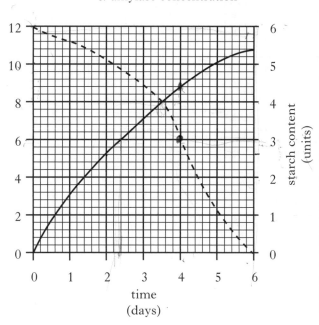

What is the α-amylase concentration when the starch content has decreased by 50%?

A   4·4 units

B   6·0 units

C   8·2 units

D   8·8 units

24. A species of plant was exposed to various periods of light and dark, after which its flowering response was observed.

The results are shown below.

Light period (hours)	Dark period (hours)	Flowering response
4	12	flowering
4	10	flowering
6	18	maximum flowering
14	10	flowering
18	9	no flowering
18	6	no flowering
18	10	flowering

What appears to be the critical factor which stimulates flowering?

A   A minimum dark period of 10 hours

B   A light/dark cycle of at least 24 hours

C   A light period of less than 18 hours

D   A dark period which exceeds the light period

25. When there is a decrease in the water concentration of the blood, which of the following series of events shows the negative feedback response of the body?

	Concentration of ADH	Permeability of kidney tubules	Volume of urine
A	increases	increases	increases
B	decreases	decreases	increases
C	increases	increases	decreases
D	decreases	increases	decreases

[Turn over

26. High levels of blood glucose can cause clouding of the lens in the human eye. Concentrations above 5·5 mM are believed to put the individual at a high risk of lens damage.

In an investigation, people of different ages each drank a glucose solution. The concentration of glucose in their blood was monitored over a number of hours. The results are shown in the graph below.

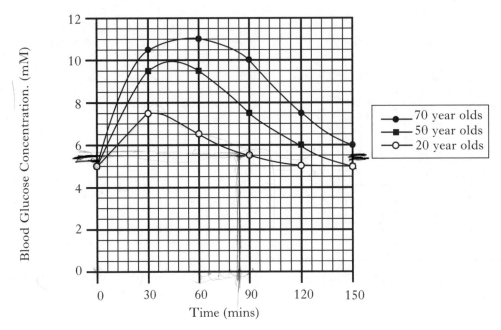

For how long during the investigation did 20 year olds remain above the high risk blood glucose concentration?

A 84 mins

B 90 mins

C 120 mins

D 148 mins

27. Which of the following shows correct responses to changes in sugar concentration in the blood?

	Sugar concentration in blood	Glucagon secretion	Insulin secretion	Glycogen stored in liver
A	increases	decreases	increases	increases
B	increases	decreases	increases	decreases
C	decreases	increases	decreases	increases
D	decreases	decreases	increases	decreases

28. A person produces 0·75 litres of urine in 24 hours. This urine contains 18 g of urea.

What is the concentration of urea in this urine?

A 1·0 g/100 cm^3

B 2·4 g/litre

C 2·4 g/100 cm^3

D 3·6 g/100 cm^3

29. The list below describes changes involved in temperature regulation.

List

1 Increased vasodilation

2 Decreased vasodilation

3 Hair erector muscles contract

4 Hair erector muscles relax

Which of these are responses to cooling in mammals?

A 1 and 3 only

B 1 and 4 only

C 2 and 3 only

D 2 and 4 only

30. Which line in the table below shows correctly the main source of body heat and the method of controlling body temperature in an ectotherm?

	Main source of body heat	Method of controlling body temperature
A	Respiration	Physiological
B	Respiration	Behavioural
C	Absorbed from environment	Physiological
D	Absorbed from environment	Behavioural

Candidates are reminded that the answer sheet MUST be returned INSIDE the front cover of this answer book.

[Turn over

Marks

SECTION B

All questions in this section should be attempted.

All answers must be written clearly and legibly in ink.

1. (*a*) The diagram below shows light striking a green leaf.

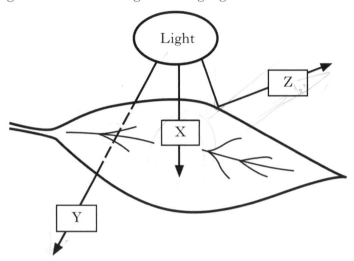

Arrow X shows light being absorbed.

State the terms used to describe what is happening to light at Y and Z.

Y ___transmitted___

Z ___reflected___   1

(*b*) The diagram below represents the absorption of different colours of light by a photosynthetic pigment.

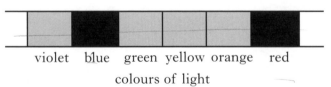

violet   blue   green   yellow   orange   red

colours of light

⬛ high absorption

⬜ low absorption

(i) Name this photosynthetic pigment.

___chlorophyll a___   1

(ii) State the role of accessory pigments in photosynthesis.

___pigments pass on energy and___

___absorb. diff___   1

Marks

1.   **(continued)**

(c)   The diagram below shows an outline of the carbon fixation stage of photosynthesis.

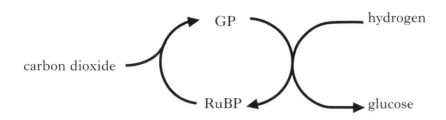

(i)   State the exact location of this stage in a plant cell.

_____   **1**

(ii)   Describe the role of hydrogen in the carbon fixation stage.

_____

_____   **1**

(d)   The graph below shows the effect of increasing the concentration of carbon dioxide on the rate of photosynthesis by a plant at different temperatures.

Light intensity was kept constant.

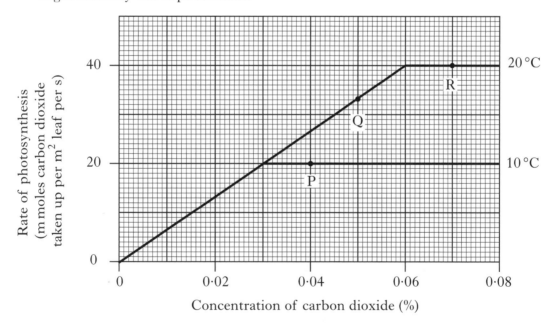

Concentration of carbon dioxide (%)

Using the information in the graph, identify the factor which is limiting the rate of photosynthesis at each of the points P, Q and R.

P _____

Q _____

R _____   **2**

Marks

2. (*a*) The diagram below shows some of the steps in respiration.

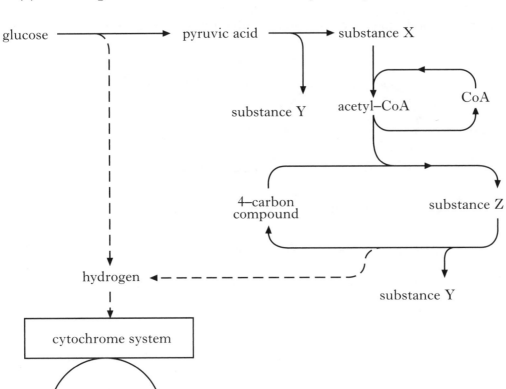

(i) Complete the table below by naming substances W, X and Y.

Substance	*Name*
W	O_2
X	acelyle grap
Y	CO_2

2

(ii) State the number of carbon atoms present in a molecule of substance Z.

_____

1

Marks

2.   (continued)

(*b*) Yeast cells were grown in both aerobic and anaerobic conditions and the volume of carbon dioxide produced was measured.

The results are shown in the graph below.

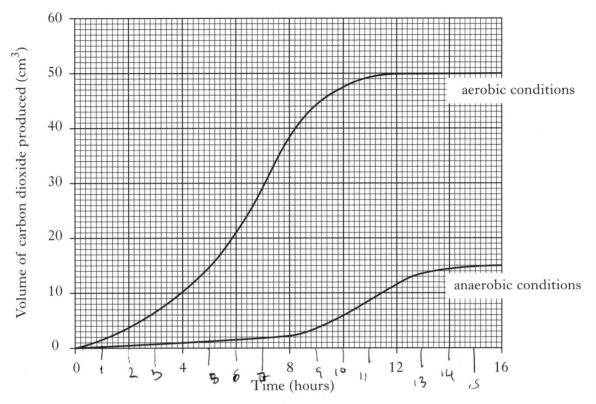

(i)   At which time is there the greatest difference between the volumes of carbon dioxide produced in aerobic and anaerobic conditions?

Tick (✓) the correct box.

☐   ☐   ☐   ☐   ☐

8 hours   10 hours   12 hours   14 hours   16 hours   1

(ii) Calculate the average rate of carbon dioxide production per hour over the first 6 hours in aerobic conditions.

Space for calculation

_____ cm³ per hour   1

[Turn over

Marks

3. (*a*) The diagram below shows one stage in the synthesis of a protein at a ribosome.

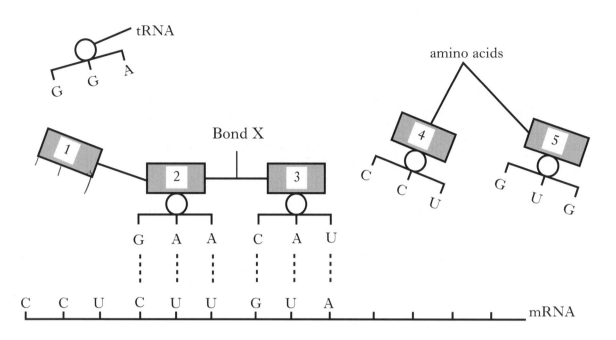

(i) Name this stage in protein synthesis.

translation

1

(ii) Name bond X.

peptide

1

(iii) The table below shows five codons and their corresponding amino acids.

Codon	Amino acid
CUU	leucine
GGA	glycine
CAA	glutamic acid
GUA	valine
CCU	proline

Use information from the table to identify amino acids 1 and 4.

1 _____*glycine*_____

4 _____*proline*_____

1

Marks

3. **(continued)**

(*b*) The diagram below shows a cell from the pancreas.

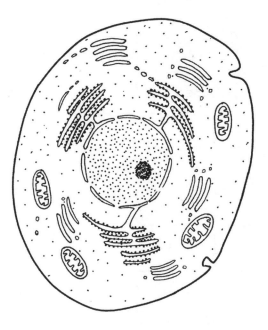

What feature of this cell shows that it is involved in the secretion of protein?

_____   1

[Turn over

Marks

4. (*a*) The diagram below shows some stages during the invasion of a cell by a virus.

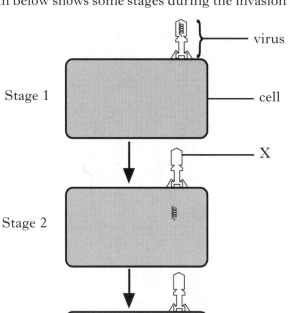

(i) Name the substance of which part X is composed.

_____ proten _____ **1**

(ii) Describe what happens in the cell between stage 2 and stage 3 to allow the viral nucleic acid to replicate.

_____

_____ **1**

(iii) Describe **two** events which occur between stage 3 and the bursting of the cell to release new viruses.

1 _____

_____

2 _____

_____ **2**

Marks

4. **(continued)**

(*b*) The presence of viruses in the human body triggers antibody production by lymphocytes.

   (i) What name is given to any substance that triggers this response?

_____ **1**

   (ii) A person was injected with a vaccine on day 1 and again on day 36 of a 70 day study. The table below shows the concentration of antibodies to this vaccine in this person's blood at the end of each 7 day period during the study.

1st injection   2nd injection

Day	7	14	21	28	35	42	49	56	63	70
Concentration of antibody (mg/100 ml blood)	3	15	28	32	10	80	102	112	120	118

    1 How many times greater was the maximum antibody concentration following the second injection compared with the maximum concentration following the first?

    Space for calculation

_____ times **1**

    2 The second injection caused a higher concentration of antibody to be produced than the first injection.

    Identify **two** other differences in the response to the second injection.

    1 _____

    2 _____ **1**

[Turn over

Marks

5. Mexican spotted owls are territorial and prey on several species of small mammal.
    Three pairs of owls were studied over a two year period.

    The table below shows the number of each prey species eaten by each pair of owls.

Prey species	Number of each prey species eaten by each pair of owls		
	Owl pair A	Owl pair B	Owl pair C
deer mouse	484	528	515
woodrat	29	144	141
brush mouse	15	114	118
rock squirrel	22	24	23

The graph below shows the average number and average total biomass of deer mice and woodrats living in the study area in different seasons.

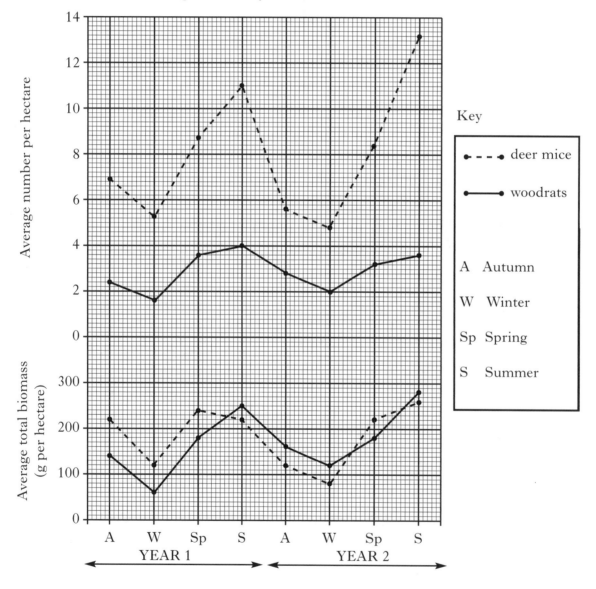

Key

- - - ● deer mice

●——● woodrats

A   Autumn

W   Winter

Sp Spring

S   Summer

(a) (i) What percentage of the total number of prey eaten by owl pair A were
         deer mice?

         Space for calculation

_____ %   **1**

5. **(*a*)** **(continued)**

Marks

(ii) Express as the simplest whole number ratio the numbers of deer mice, brush mice and rock squirrels eaten by owl pair B.

Space for calculation

deer mice   :   brush mice   :   rock squirrels

_____ : _____ : _____   1

(*b*) Use evidence from the table to identify the owl pair that foraged in a different habitat to the other two pairs of owls.

Justify your answer.

Pair_____

Justification _____

_____

_____   1

(*c*) (i) **Use values from the graph** to describe the change in average number of woodrats per hectare from spring of Year 1 until spring of Year 2.

_____

_____   2

(ii) Calculate the percentage decrease in the average total biomass of woodrats between summer of Year 1 and winter of Year 2.

Space for calculation

_____ %   1

(*d*) Calculate the average biomass of one deer mouse in summer of Year 1.

Space for calculation

_____ g   1

(*e*) The size of the territory of a pair of Mexican spotted owls is different in winter and summer. Give an explanation of this observation which can be supported by evidence from the graph.

_____

_____

_____   1

Marks

6. The diagram below shows a pair of homologous chromosomes in a mouse cell during meiosis. The positions of three genes R, S and T are also shown.

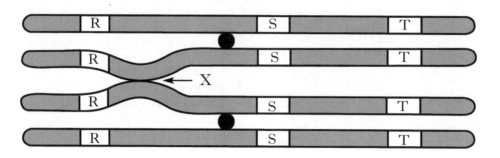

(a) Name an organ in mice where meiosis occurs.

_____   1

(b) (i) Name point X where crossing over may occur.

_____   1

(ii) Crossing over leads to recombination of genes.

Between which two genes in the diagram would the greatest frequency of recombination take place?

_____ and _____   1

(iii) Crossing over is a source of genetic variation.

Name **one** other feature of meiosis which leads to genetic variation.

_____   1

(c) A mouse egg contains 20 chromosomes.

State the number of chromosomes present in a mouse gamete mother cell.

_____ chromosomes   1

Marks

7. In Labrador dogs, the alleles **B** and **b** and alleles **E** and **e** are involved in the determination of coat colour.

- Labradors with alleles **B** and **E** are always black.

- Labradors with alleles **bb** and **E** are always chocolate coloured.

- Labradors with alleles **ee** are always yellow.

(a) A male black Labrador of genotype **BbEe** was crossed with a yellow female of the genotype **bbee**.

  (i) Complete the table below to show the genotypes of the gametes of the male.

Genotypes of male gametes			

1

  (ii) Give the expected phenotype ratio of the offspring from this cross.

Space for calculation

_____ Black : _____ Chocolate :_____ Yellow   **1**

(b) Give the genotype of a male Labrador which could be crossed with a female of genotype **bbee** to ensure that **all** the offspring produced would be chocolate coloured.

Space for calculation

Genotype _____   **1**

[Turn over

Marks

8. Cuticles are waxy layers on the surfaces of the leaves of many plant species.

    The table below shows the average cuticle thickness of the leaves of five plant species and the rates of water loss through their cuticles at 20 °C with no air movement.

Species	Average cuticle thickness (micrometres)	Rate of water loss through cuticle (cubic micrometres per cm^2 per hour)
A	1·4	36·7
B	2·8	25·8
C	4·2	18·1
D	5·6	8·5
E	7·0	8·4

(a) (i) Describe the relationship between average cuticle thickness and rate of water loss through the cuticles in these plant species.

_____

_____

_____ 2

(ii) Leaves lose most water through their open stomata.

Give the term used to describe the condition of the guard cells when stomata are open.

_____ 1

(iii) State **two** changes to environmental conditions which could lead to an increase in water loss from leaves.

1 _____

2 _____ 1

Marks

8. **(continued)**

(b) Plants which grow in extremely dry conditions have leaf adaptations which reduce water loss.

(i) Complete the table below to explain how each leaf adaptation reduces water loss.

Leaf adaptation	*Explanation of how the adaptation reduces water loss from leaves*
Presence of hairs on leaf surface	
Leaves small and few in number	

2

(ii) What term describes plants that have adaptations to reduce water loss?

_____

1

[Turn over

Marks

9. (*a*) In an investigation into the effects of grazing, the total biomass of grass species and the diversity of all plant species in a field was monitored over a period of four years. The field was not grazed in years 1 and 2. Sheep grazed the field in years 3 and 4.

The results are shown on the graph below.

- - - - diversity   ———— biomass

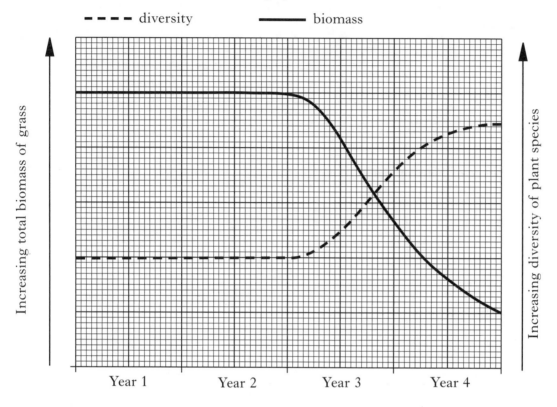

(i)   Explain the effects of grazing by sheep on the total biomass of grass species and the diversity of plant species during year 3.

Total biomass of grass species.

_____   1

Diversity of all plant species

_____

_____   1

(ii) The number of sheep grazing the field was increased after year 4. Suggest how this would affect the diversity of plant species in the field.

Justify your answer.

Effect on diversity

_____

Justification

_____

_____   1

DO NOT WRITE IN THIS MARGIN

Marks

9. (continued)

(*b*) The table below contains statements describing plant adaptations.

Complete the table by ticking (✓) the boxes to show the adaptations that help the plants tolerate the effects of grazing.

Plant adaptation	*Tick (✓)*
Dandelions have deep roots	
Wild roses have thorns	
Couch grass has underground stems	
Nettles have stings	
Tobacco plants produce nicotine	

2

[Turn over

Marks

10. Catechol oxidase is an enzyme found in apple tissue. It is involved in the reaction which produces the brown pigment that forms in cut or damaged apples.

catechol   catechol oxidase
(colourless substance $\longrightarrow$ brown pigments
in apple tissue)

The effect of the concentration of lead ethanoate on this reaction was investigated.

10 g of apple tissue was cut up, added to $10\,cm^3$ of distilled water and then liquidised and filtered. This produced an extract containing both catechol and catechol oxidase.

Test tubes were set up as described in **Table 1** and kept at 20 °C in a water bath.

Table 1

Tube	Contents of tubes
A	sample of extract + $1\,cm^3$ distilled water
B	sample of extract + $1\,cm^3$ 0·01% lead ethanoate solution
C	sample of extract + $1\,cm^3$ 0·1% lead ethanoate solution

Every 10 minutes, the tubes were placed in a colorimeter which measured how much brown pigment was present.

The more brown pigment present the higher the colorimeter reading.

The results are shown in **Table 2**.

Table 2

Time (minutes)	Colorimeter reading (units)		
	Tube A	Tube B	Tube C
	sample of extract + distilled water	sample of extract + 0·01% lead ethanoate	sample of extract + 0·1% lead ethanoate
0	1·6	1·8	1·6
10	7·0	5·0	2·0
20	9·0	6·0	2·2
30	9·6	6·4	2·4
40	10·0	7·0	2·4
50	10·0	7·6	2·4
60	10·0	7·6	2·4

(a) (i) Identify **two** variables not already mentioned that would have to be kept constant.

1 _____ 1

2 _____ 1

Marks

10. **(*a*) (continued)**

(ii) Describe how tube A acts as a control in this investigation.

_____

_____ 1

(*b*) Explain why the initial colorimeter readings were not 0·0 units.

_____

_____ 1

(*c*) The results for the extract with 0·1% lead ethanoate are shown in the graph below.

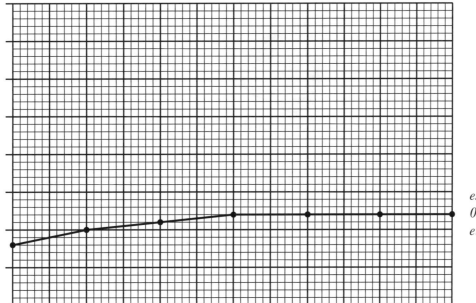

*extract +
0·1% lead
ethanoate*

Use information from **Table 2** to complete the graph by:

(i) adding the scale and label to each axis; 1

(ii) presenting the results for the extract + 0·01% lead ethanoate solution **and** labelling the line. 1

(Additional graph paper, if required, will be found on page 40.)

(*d*) State the effect of the concentration of lead ethanoate solution on the activity of catechol oxidase.

_____

_____ 1

(*e*) The experiment was repeated with the 0·1% lead ethanoate solution at 60 °C. Predict the colorimeter reading at 10 minutes and justify your answer.

Prediction _____ units

Justification _____

_____ 1

Marks

11. Many species of cichlid fish are found in Lake Malawi in Africa.

    The diagram below shows the heads of three different cichlid fish and gives information on their feeding methods.

    These species have evolved from a single species.

Sucks in microscopic
organisms from the water

Scrapes algae from the
surfaces of rocks

Crushes snail shells and
extracts flesh

(a) Describe how the information given about these fish illustrates adaptive radiation.

_____

_____

_____   2

(b) What evidence would confirm that the cichlids are different species?

_____

_____   1

(c) The evolution of these cichlid fish has involved geographical isolation.

    (i) Name another type of isolating mechanism.

    _____   1

    (ii) State the importance of isolating mechanisms in the evolution of new species.

    _____

    _____   1

Marks

12. Diagram A shows a section through a woody stem. Diagram B shows a magnified view of the area indicated on the section.

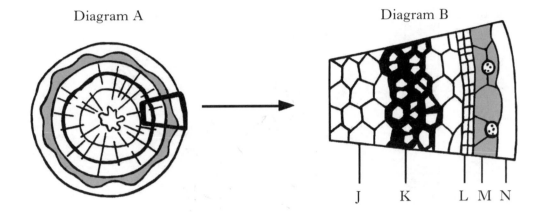

Diagram A   Diagram B

                                                    J   K   L M N

(a) Which letter on diagram B shows the position of a lateral meristem?

Letter _____   **1**

(b) Name the tissue of which annual rings are composed.

_____   **1**

(c) In which season was the woody stem cut?
Explain your choice.

Season _____   **1**

Explanation _____

_____

_____   **1**

[Turn over

Marks

13. The diagram below shows information relating to the Jacob–Monod hypothesis of the control of gene action in the bacterium *Escherichia coli*.

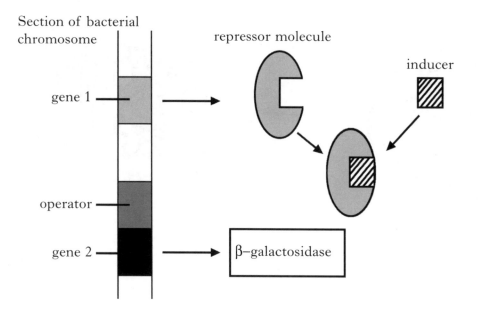

(a) Name gene 1.

regulator gene

1

(b) Name the substance which acts as the inducer.

Lactose

1

(c) (i) Describe the sequence of events that occurs in the **absence** of the inducer.

The repressor protein binds to the operator so the operator is occupied and gene structural gene switched off → No B-galactosidase

2

(ii) Explain why it is important for *E. coli* to control gene action.

So there is no wasted conversion & this saves energy

1

DO NOT WRITE IN THIS MARGIN

Marks

14. Environmental factors influence growth and development in animals.

(*a*) (i) Explain the importance of iron in the growth and development of humans.

____

____ **1**

(ii) Describe the effects of nicotine on growth and development of a human fetus.

____

____ **1**

(*b*) Breeding behaviour in red deer starts in autumn.

(i) Describe the environmental influence that triggers the start of breeding at this time of year.

____

____ **1**

(ii) Suggest an advantage to red deer of starting to breed at this time of year.

____

____ **1**

[Turn over

Marks

15. The diagram below shows the plant communities that have developed around a fresh water loch.

Increasing age of communities ➤

(*a*) What term describes the process of gradual formation of a climax community?

_____   1

(*b*) Suggest a modification that community X may make to its habitat which allows colonisation by community Y.

_____

_____   1

(*c*) **Underline** one alternative in each pair to make the sentences correct.

The complexity of the food web in the climax community will be

$\left\{ \begin{array}{l} \text{greater than} \\ \text{less than} \end{array} \right\}$ that in the pioneer community.

Greater species diversity will exist in $\left\{ \begin{array}{l} \text{community X} \\ \text{community Y} \end{array} \right\}$.   1

SECTION C

Both questions in this section should be attempted.

Note that each question contains a choice.

Questions 1 and 2 should be attempted on the blank pages which follow.

Supplementary sheets, if required, may be obtained from the invigilator.

All answers must be written clearly and legibly in ink.

Labelled diagrams may be used where appropriate.

Marks

1. Answer **either** A **or** B.

   A. Write notes on:

      (i)   structure of the plasma membrane;   **4**

      (ii)   function of the plasma membrane in active transport;   **3**

      (iii)   structure and function of the cell wall.   **3**

      (10)

   OR

   B. Write notes on :

      (i)   the structure of DNA;   **6**

      (ii)   DNA replication and its importance.   **4**

      (10)

In question 2, ONE mark is available for coherence and ONE mark is available for relevance.

2. Answer **either** A **or** B.

   A. Give an account of the importance of nitrogen, phosphorus and magnesium in plant growth and describe the symptoms of their deficiency.   **(10)**

   OR

   B. Give an account of how animal populations are regulated by density-dependent and by density-independent factors.   **(10)**

[END OF QUESTION PAPER]

[Turn over

SPACE FOR ANSWERS

SPACE FOR ANSWERS

SPACE FOR ANSWERS

SPACE FOR ANSWERS

SPACE FOR ANSWERS

SPACE FOR ANSWERS

SPACE FOR ANSWERS

ADDITIONAL GRAPH PAPER FOR QUESTION 10(*c*)

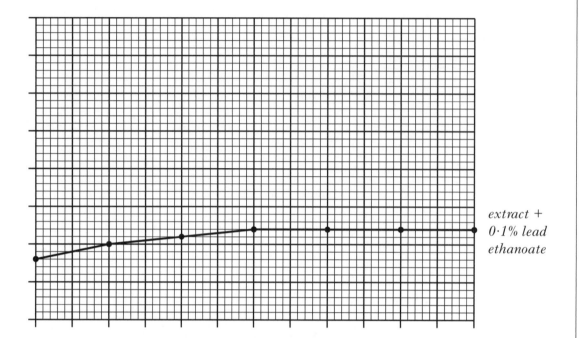

*extract +
0·1% lead
ethanoate*

HIGHER

2010

[BLANK PAGE]

FOR OFFICIAL USE

Total for
Sections
B and C

X007/301

NATIONAL
QUALIFICATIONS
2010

THURSDAY, 27 MAY
1.00 PM – 3.30 PM

BIOLOGY
HIGHER

Fill in these boxes and read what is printed below.

Full name of centre

Town

Forename(s)

Surname

Date of birth

Day	Month	Year	Scottish candidate number	Number of seat

SECTION A—Questions 1–30 (30 marks)

Instructions for completion of Section A are given on page two.

For this section of the examination you must use an **HB pencil**.

SECTIONS B AND C (100 marks)

1 (a) All questions should be attempted.

   (b) It should be noted that in **Section C** questions 1 and 2 each contain a choice.

2 The questions may be answered in any order but all answers are to be written in the spaces provided in this answer book, **and must be written clearly and legibly in ink**.

3 Additional space for answers will be found at the end of the book. If further space is required, supplementary sheets may be obtained from the Invigilator and should be inserted inside the **front** cover of this book.

4 The numbers of questions must be clearly inserted with any answers written in the additional space.

5 Rough work, if any should be necessary, should be written in this book and then scored through when the fair copy has been written. If further space is required a supplementary sheet for rough work may be obtained from the Invigilator.

6 Before leaving the examination room you must give this book to the Invigilator. If you do not, you may lose all the marks for this paper.

Read carefully

1   Check that the answer sheet provided is for **Biology Higher (Section A)**.

2   For this section of the examination you must use an **HB pencil**, and where necessary, an eraser.

3   Check that the answer sheet you have been given has **your name**, **date of birth**, **SCN** (Scottish Candidate Number) and **Centre Name** printed on it.

    Do not change any of these details.

4   If any of this information is wrong, tell the Invigilator immediately.

5   If this information is correct, **print** your name and seat number in the boxes provided.

6   The answer to each question is **either** A, B, C or D. Decide what your answer is, then, using your pencil, put a horizontal line in the space provided (see sample question below).

7   There is **only one correct** answer to each question.

8   Any rough working should be done on the question paper or the rough working sheet, **not** on your answer sheet.

9   At the end of the examination, put the **answer sheet for Section A inside the front cover of this answer book**.

Sample Question

The apparatus used to determine the energy stored in a foodstuff is a

A   calorimeter

B   respirometer

C   klinostat

D   gas burette.

The correct answer is **A**—calorimeter. The answer **A** has been clearly marked in **pencil** with a horizontal line (see below).

Changing an answer

If you decide to change your answer, carefully erase your first answer and using your pencil fill in the answer you want. The answer below has been changed to **D**.

SECTION A

All questions in this section should be attempted.

Answers should be given on the separate answer sheet provided.

1. The diagram below represents an osmosis experiment, using a model cell.

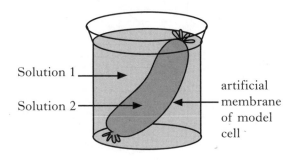

Solution 1

Solution 2

artificial membrane of model cell

Which line of the table below shows a correct result for the solutions used in the experiment?

	Solution 1	Solution 2	Change of volume in model cell
A	water	5% sucrose	decrease
B	10% sucrose	water	increase
C	10% sucrose	5% sucrose	increase
D	10% sucrose	15% sucrose	increase

2. The cells of seaweed which actively absorb iodide ions from sea water would be expected to have large numbers of

   A chloroplasts

   B mitochondria

   C ribosomes

   D vacuoles.

3. An investigation was carried out into the uptake of sodium ions by animal cells. The graph below shows the rates of sodium ion uptake and breakdown of glucose at different concentrations of oxygen.

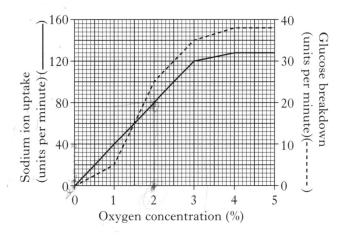

How many units of sodium ions are taken up over a 5 minute period when the concentration of oxygen in solution is 2%?

   A 80

   B 100

   C 400

   D 500

4. Which line in the table below correctly shows the two chemical reactions which occur in the grana of a chloroplast following the absorption of light energy by chlorophyll?

	Chemical reaction 1	Chemical reaction 2
A	ATP → ADP + Pi	water → hydrogen + oxygen
B	ADP + Pi → ATP	water → hydrogen + oxygen
C	ATP → ADP + Pi	hydrogen + oxygen → water
D	ADP + Pi → ATP	hydrogen + oxygen → water

5. Which line in the table below correctly shows the number of molecules of ATP used and produced when one molecule of glucose undergoes glycolysis?

	Number of molecules of ATP	
	Used	Produced
A	0	2
B	2	0
C	2	4
D	4	2

6. The graphs below show the results of an experiment into the effect of aerobic and anaerobic conditions on the uptake of calcium and magnesium ions by pond algae.

Uptake of calcium ions by pond algae

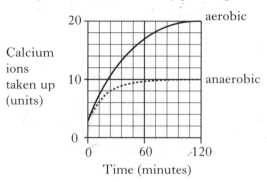

Uptake of magnesium ions by pond algae

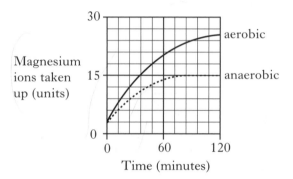

Which of the following is a valid conclusion that can be drawn from the results?

A At 120 minutes in aerobic conditions the uptake of calcium ions is greater than that of magnesium ions.

B At 60 minutes in anaerobic conditions there was a greater uptake of calcium ions compared with magnesium ions.

C Over the 120 minutes in aerobic conditions the average rate of uptake of calcium ions is greater than that of magnesium ions.

D At 60 minutes in anaerobic conditions there was a greater uptake of magnesium ions compared with calcium ions.

7. The table below refers to processes in cellular respiration.

Process	Carbon dioxide produced	Water produced
X	no	no
Y	yes	no
Z	no	yes

Which line in the table below correctly identifies processes X, Y and Z?

	X	Y	Z
A	glycolysis	Krebs cycle	cytochrome system
B	Krebs cycle	glycolysis	cytochrome system
C	cytochrome system	Krebs cycle	glycolysis
D	glycolysis	cytochrome system	Krebs cycle

8. The diagram below represents the chemical structure of the protein ADH.

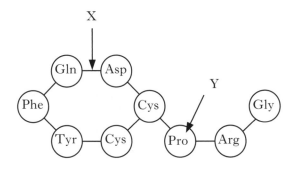

Which line in the table below identifies X and Y correctly?

	X	Y
A	hydrogen bond	base
B	hydrogen bond	amino acid
C	peptide bond	base
D	peptide bond	amino acid

9. A fragment of DNA was found to have 120 guanine bases and 60 adenine bases. What is the total number of sugar molecules in this fragment?

A   60

B   90

C   180

D   360

10. Which of the following statements about viruses is true?

A   Viral protein directs the synthesis of new viruses.

B   New viruses are assembled outside the host cell.

C   Viral protein is injected into the host cell.

D   Viral DNA directs the synthesis of new viruses.

11. Which line in the table below correctly describes the cells produced by meiosis?

	Cells produced by meiosis	
	Chromosome complement	Genetic composition
A	haploid	all cells different
B	diploid	all cells identical
C	diploid	all cells different
D	haploid	all cells identical

[Turn over

12. In mice, coat length is determined by the dominant allele **L** for long coat and the recessive allele **l** for short coat.

Coat colour is determined by the dominant allele for brown colour **B** and recessive allele for white colour **b**.

The genes are not linked.

What proportion of the offspring produced from a cross between two mice heterozygous for coat length and colour would have short brown coats?

A   1 in 16

B   3 in 16

C   9 in 16

D   1 in 4

13. Cystic fibrosis is an inherited condition caused by a recessive allele. The diagram below shows a family tree with affected individuals.

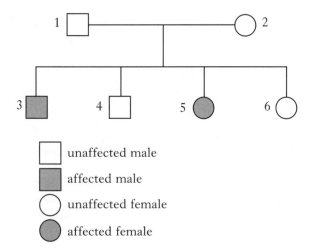

☐ unaffected male

■ affected male

○ unaffected female

● affected female

Which individuals in this family tree **must** be heterozygous for this condition?

A   3 and 5

B   4 and 6

C   1 and 2

D   2 and 6

14. In *Drosophila*, wings can be straight or curly and body colour can be black or grey.

Heterozygous flies with straight wings and black bodies were crossed with curly-winged and grey bodied flies.

The following results were obtained.

Number	797	806	85	89
Phenotype	straight wings and black bodies	curly wings and grey bodies	straight wings and grey bodies	curly wings and black bodies

These proportions of offspring suggest that

A   genes for body colour and wing shape are on separate chromosomes

B   crossing over has caused linked genes to separate

C   the genes show independent assortment

D   the genes must be carried on the sex chromosomes.

15. The diagram below represents the evolution of bread wheat. The diploid chromosome numbers of the species involved are given.

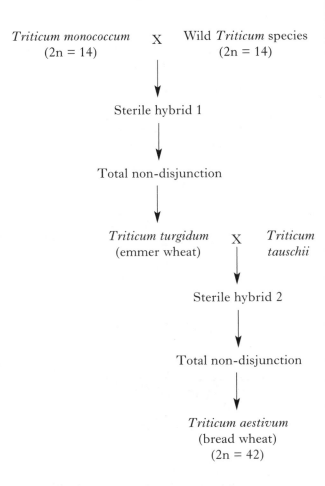

Triticum monococcum   X   Wild *Triticum* species
(2n = 14)   (2n = 14)

Sterile hybrid 1

Total non-disjunction

Triticum turgidum   X   *Triticum*
(emmer wheat)   *tauschii*

Sterile hybrid 2

Total non-disjunction

Triticum aestivum
(bread wheat)
(2n = 42)

Which line in the table below identifies correctly the diploid chromosome numbers of *Triticum turgidum* (emmer wheat) and *Triticum tauschii*?

	Triticum turgidum	*Triticum tauschii*
A	14	14
B	28	14
C	14	28
D	28	28

16. The flow chart below represents the programming of *E. coli* bacteria to produce human insulin.

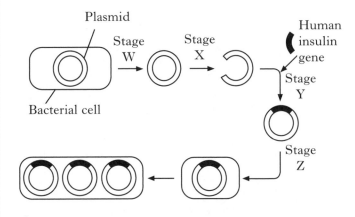

Which line in the table below identifies correctly the stages at which an endonuclease and a ligase are used?

	Endonuclease	*Ligase*
A	Stage X	Stage W
B	Stage Y	Stage Z
C	Stage X	Stage Y
D	Stage Y	Stage X

17. Which of the following statements could be **true** of cooperative hunting?

1 Individuals gain more energy than from hunting alone.

2 Both dominant and subordinate animals benefit.

3 Much larger prey may be killed than by hunting alone.

A   1 and 2 only

B   1 and 3 only

C   2 and 3 only

D   1, 2 and 3

[Turn over

18. The table below shows the mass of water gained and lost by a small mammal over a 24-hour period.

	Mass of water lost or gained (g)
Food	6
Metabolic water	54
Exhaled air	45
Urine	12
Faeces	3

What percentage of water gained comes from metabolic water?

A   9%

B   45%

C   54%

D   90%

19. The graph below shows the relationship between the ratio of body masses of two male fish and the average time they spend fighting for territory.

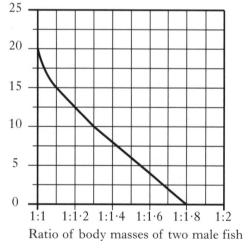

For how long will a fight between two fish, weighing 6 g and 9 g respectively, be expected to last?

A   6 minutes

B   10 minutes

C   15 minutes

D   17 minutes

20. Increased grazing by herbivores in a grassland habitat can result in an increase in the number of different plant species present in the habitat.

This is because

A   some plants tolerate grazing because they have low meristems

B   damage to dominant grasses by grazing allows the survival of other species

C   grasses can regenerate quickly following damage by herbivores

D   many grassland species produce toxins in response to grazing.

21. The diagram below shows a section of a woody twig.

Which is a region of summer wood?

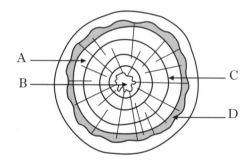

22. According to the Jacob-Monod hypothesis, a regulator gene is responsible for

A   coding for the production of an inducer molecule

B   switching on an operator

C   coding for the production of a repressor molecule

D   switching on a structural gene.

23. The graph below shows the effect of photoperiod on the onset of flowering in a species of plant.

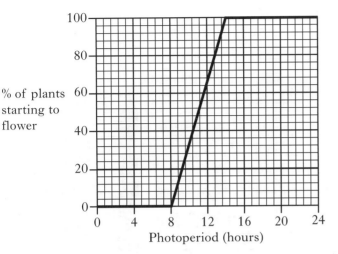

Photoperiod (hours)

The graph shows that the plant is a

A   long day species with a critical photoperiod of 8 hours

B   long day species with a critical photoperiod of 14 hours

C   short day species with a critical photoperiod of 8 hours

D   short day species with a critical photoperiod of 14 hours.

24. The following list shows the effects of drugs on fetal development in humans.

1   Limb deformation

2   Overall reduction of growth

3   Slowing of mental development

Which line in the table below correctly matches alcohol, nicotine and thalidomide with their effects on fetal development?

	Alcohol	Nicotine	Thalidomide
A	2 only	2 and 3 only	1 and 3 only
B	3 only	2 and 3 only	1 only
C	2 and 3 only	2 only	1 and 3 only
D	2 and 3 only	2 and 3 only	1 only

25. Which line in the table below identifies correctly the hormones which stimulate the conversion of glucose and glycogen?

	glycogen → glucose	glucose → glycogen
A	glucagon and adrenalin	insulin
B	adrenalin	glucagon and insulin
C	insulin	adrenalin and glucagon
D	glucagon and insulin	adrenalin

26. Drinking a large volume of water will lead to

A   increased production of ADH and kidney tubules becoming more permeable to water

B   decreased production of ADH and kidney tubules becoming less permeable to water

C   increased production of ADH and kidney tubules becoming less permeable to water

D   decreased production of ADH and kidney tubules becoming more permeable to water.

[Turn over

27. The graph below shows how the concentration of insulin in the blood varies with the concentration of glucose in the blood.

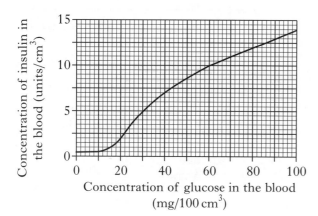

What total mass of glucose would be present at an insulin concentration of 10 units/cm^3, in an individual with 5 litres of blood?

A   60 mg

B   300 mg

C   3000 mg

D   6000 mg

28. The graph below shows the annual variation in the biomass and population density of *Corophium*, a small burrowing invertebrate found in the mud of most Scottish estuaries.

Key

☐ = Biomass

■ = Population density

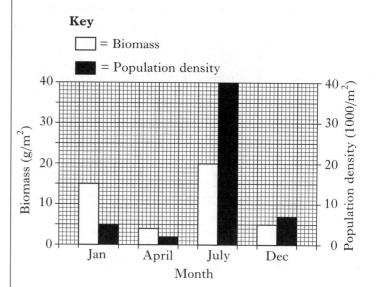

During which month do individual *Corophium* have the greatest average mass?

A   January

B   April

C   July

D   December

29. The graph below shows the effect of air temperature on the metabolic rate of two different animals.

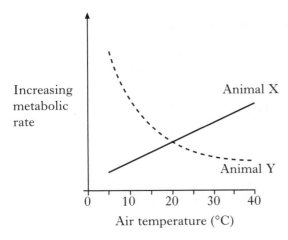

Air temperature (°C)

Which line in the table below identifies correctly the temperatures at which oxygen consumption will be greatest in the tissues of each animal?

	Animal X	Animal Y
A	20 °C	20 °C
B	40 °C	40 °C
C	40 °C	5 °C
D	5 °C	40 °C

30. Which of the following comparisons of early and late succession in plant communities in their habitat is correct?

	Early succession	Late succession
A	low biomass	high biomass
B	complex food webs	simple food webs
C	soil is deep	soil is shallow
D	high species diversity	low species diversity

Candidates are reminded that the answer sheet MUST be returned INSIDE the front cover of this answer book.

[Turn over

Marks

SECTION B

All questions in this section should be attempted.

All answers must be written clearly and legibly in ink.

1. (a) The following sentences give information about the plasma membrane of beetroot cells.

   Underline one alternative in each pair to make the sentences correct.

   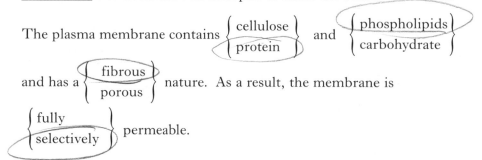

   2

   (b) Cyanide is a poison that inhibits enzymes involved in aerobic respiration.

   The graph below shows how cyanide concentration affects the uptake of chloride ions by beetroot cells.

   The rates of chloride ion uptake are given as percentages of those obtained in a control experiment with no cyanide.

   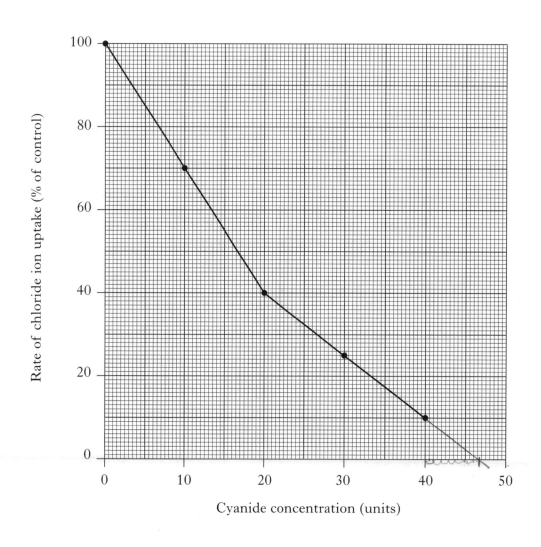

DO NOT WRITE IN THIS MARGIN

Marks

1. (*b*) (continued)

(i) Predict the cyanide concentration at which chloride ion uptake would stop.

46·5 units **1**

(ii) The rate of chloride ion uptake by beetroot at 30 units of cyanide was 200 μg per hour.

Calculate the rate of uptake in the control experiment.

Space for calculation

____________ μg per hour **1**

(iii) The uptake of chloride ions occurs by active transport.

Explain how the information given supports this statement.

____

____

____

____ **2**

[Turn over

Marks

2. (a) State the **exact** location of photosynthetic pigments in plant leaf cells.

_____grana._____   1

(b) The table below shows the mass of photosynthetic pigments in the leaves of two plant species.

Photosynthetic pigment	Mass of photosynthetic pigment in the leaves (μg per cm^3 of leaf)	
	Species A	Species B
chlorophyll a	0·92	0·93
chlorophyll b	0·34	0·35
carotene	0·32	0·65
xanthophyll	0·28	0·55

Which species is best adapted to grow in the shade of taller plants?

Explain your choice.

Species ____B____

Explanation ___They have a wider range___

___of wavelengths, plants are able___

___to._____   1

Marks

2. **(continued)**

(*c*) The diagram below shows some events in the carbon fixation stage (Calvin cycle) of photosynthesis in a plant kept in bright light.

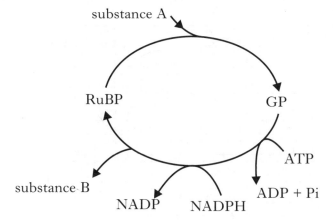

(i) Name substances A and B.

A _____ CO_2 _____

B _____ glucose _____   2

(ii) NADP carries hydrogen to the carbon fixation stage.

Describe the role of hydrogen in the carbon fixation stage.

_____

_____   1

(iii) Complete the table below to show the number of carbon atoms in one molecule of each compound.

Compound	Number of carbon atoms per molecule
RuBP	
GP	

1

(iv) Predict what would happen to the concentrations of RuBP and GP in leaf cells if the plant was moved from bright light into dark conditions.

Explain your answer.

RuBP _____

GP _____   1

Explanation _____

_____   1

Marks

3. In an investigation, yeast was grown in a glucose solution for 160 minutes in a sterilised fermenter. Temperature was kept constant and anaerobic conditions were maintained. The graph below shows the changes in concentration of ethanol in the fermenter during the period.

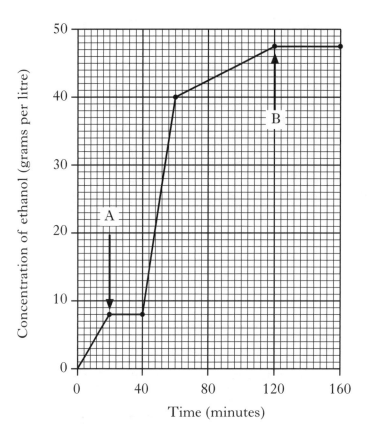

(a) (i) Calculate the increase in concentration of ethanol between 60 and 140 minutes.

Space for calculation

_____ grams per litre   **1**

(ii) Calculate the average increase in ethanol concentration per minute during the first 40 minutes.

Space for calculation

_____ grams per litre per minute   **1**

(b) (i) At point A on the graph, the ethanol concentration stopped increasing when air temporarily leaked into the fermenter.

Explain this result.

_____

_____   **2**

(ii) Assuming no further air leaks, explain why the ethanol concentration stopped increasing at point B.

_____

_____   **1**

Marks

4. *(a)* The diagram below shows part of a DNA molecule during replication.

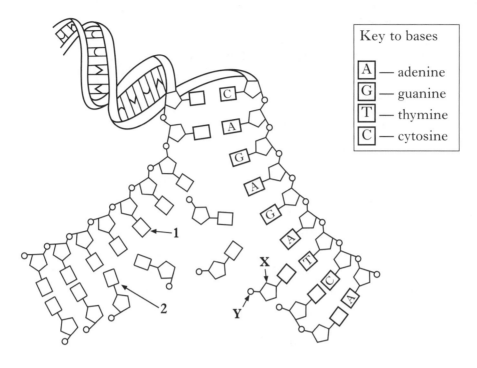

Key to bases

A — adenine
G — guanine
T — thymine
C — cytosine

(i) Identify parts X and Y.

X _deoxyribose sugar_

Y _phosphate_   1

(ii) Name bases 1 and 2.

1 _T_

2 _G_   1

(iii) Name **two** substances, not shown on the diagram, which are necessary for DNA replication.

1 _primer_

2 _DNA polymerase_   2

(iv) Name a cellular process for which DNA replication is essential.

_____   1

(b) DNA is also involved in protein synthesis.

During protein synthesis, tRNA molecules with the anticodon UAG attach to the amino acid isoleucine.

Identify the DNA base triplet which codes for isoleucine.

_____   1

Marks

5. (a) Tuberculosis is a disease caused by the bacterium *Mycobacterium tuberculosis*.

When the tuberculosis bacterium enters the human body it stimulates the production of antibodies.

   (i) Name the type of cells which produce antibodies.

   _____   1

   (ii) What term is given to any substance that stimulates antibody production?

   _____   1

(b) Leaf rust is a fungus which grows when its spores land on leaves. The fungus spreads over leaf surfaces causing damage.

Single leaves from four different species of cottonwood tree were sprayed with identical volumes of a suspension of rust fungus spores. After 3 days the percentage of leaf area with fungal growth was measured.

The tannin content in these leaves was also measured.

The results are shown in the table below.

Cottonwood species	Percentage leaf area with fungal growth after 3 days	Tannin content in leaves (mg per g of leaf dry mass)
Black	2·4	40·6
Eastern	11·4	3·9
Narrow-leafed	4·3	11·7
Swamp	3·2	15·6

   (i) Express as the simplest whole number ratio, the tannin content in the leaves of the eastern cottonwood, narrow-leafed cottonwood and swamp cottonwood.

   Space for calculation

   _____   :   _____   :   _____   1
   eastern   narrow-leafed   swamp

   (ii) Which species of cottonwood appears most resistant to attack by leaf rust fungus?

   _____   1

Marks

5. (*b*) continued

(iii) What evidence is there that tannins give protection against leaf rust fungus?

_____

_____

_____ 1

(iv) Why was the tannin content of the leaves measured in mg per g of leaf dry mass and not fresh mass?

_____

_____ 1

[Turn over

Marks

6. Honey bees are social insects. They forage for food at various distances from their hive. When a bee finds a food source, it returns to the hive and communicates the location of the food to other bees using body movements called waggle dances. These are performed several times with short intervals between them.

In an investigation, bees were fitted with radio tracking devices which allowed the distances they travelled from the hive to be measured. The waggle dances performed by each returning bee were studied. The average time taken for its waggle dance was recorded and the number of times it was performed in 15 seconds was counted.

The results are shown in the graph below.

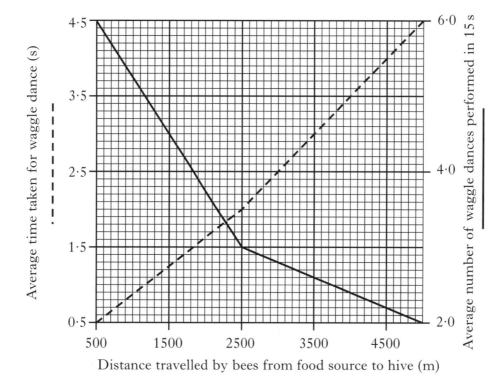

(a) (i) **Use values from the graph** to describe the relationship between the distance travelled by a bee from the food source and the number of waggle dances performed in 15 s.

_____

_____

_____   2

(ii) State the average time taken for a waggle dance when the distance travelled by a bee from the food source is 1500 m.

_____ s   1

Marks

6. (*a*) (continued)

(iii) Calculate the percentage increase in the average time taken for a waggle dance when the distance from the food source to the hive increases from 500 to 3500 metres.

Space for calculation

_____ %   **1**

(iv) Predict the total time a bee would spend in the waggle dances in a 15 s period when the food source is 2500 m away from the hive.

_____ s   **1**

(*b*) In another investigation, the waggle dances of six bees from another hive were observed.

The results are shown in the table below.

BEE	*Number of times waggle dance was performed in 15 s*
1	2·65
2	2·20
3	2·30
4	2·55
5	2·70
6	2·60
Average	

(i) Complete the table by calculating the average number of times the waggle dance was performed in 15 s.

Space for calculation

1

(ii) Using information from the table and the graph, predict the distance that was travelled by bee 6 to its food source.

_____ m   **1**

(*c*) (i) Apart from its distance from the hive, what other information about food sources would be useful to the bees?

_____   **1**

(ii) In terms of the economics of foraging, explain the advantage of waggle dances to bees.

_____

_____   **1**

Marks

7.   The diagram below shows a pair of homologous chromosomes during meiosis. P and Q show points where crossing over **may** occur. The other letters show the positions of the alleles of four genes.

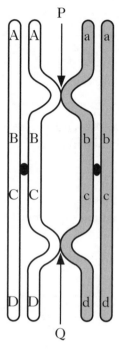

(*a*)   What evidence confirms that these chromosomes are homologous?

_____

_____   1

(*b*)   (i)   What name is given to points P and Q?

_____   1

(ii)   State the importance of crossing over in meiosis.

_____

_____   1

Marks

7. **(continued)**

(*c*)   (i)   In the table below, tick (✓) the boxes to identify which combination of alleles would result from crossing over at point P only or crossing over at both points P and Q on the diagram.

Combination of alleles	Crossing over at	
	point P only	*both points P and Q*
Abcd		
aBCD		
AbcD		
aBCd		

1

(ii)   Give **one** possible sequence of alleles which could be found in a recombinant gamete formed if crossing over occurred at point Q only.

_____

1

[Turn over

Marks

8. (a) A rare form of rickets in humans is caused by a sex-linked allele **R** which is **dominant** to the allele **r**.

   (i) Complete the table below by inserting **all** possible genotypes of the female phenotypes of this allele.

Phenotype	*Genotype(s)*
Affected female	
Unaffected female	
Affected male	$X^R Y$
Unaffected male	$X^r Y$

   2

   (ii) An affected female, whose father was unaffected, and an unaffected male have a son.

   What is the percentage chance that their son will be unaffected?

   Space for working

   _____ % chance   1

   (iii) The occurrence of allele **R** is due to a mutation in which the DNA triplet CAG is altered to TAG.

   Name this type of gene mutation and describe its effect on the structure of the protein it codes for.

   Name _____   1

   Description _____

   _____   1

(b) Rickets can also result from a deficiency of vitamin D in the diet.

   State the role of vitamin D in humans.

   _____

   _____   1

Marks

9. (a) The table below refers to environmental problems that salt water bony fish and desert rats have in osmoregulation and adaptations that these animals use to maintain their water balance.

Complete the table by giving an environmental problem faced by salt water bony fish and adding **one** adaptation to each empty box.

Animal	Environmental problem	Adaptations for maintaining water balance	
		behavioural	*physiological*
Salt water bony fish		drinks sea water	
Desert rat	little drinking water available		

2

(b) The diagram below shows a section through a floating leaf of a hydrophyte plant.

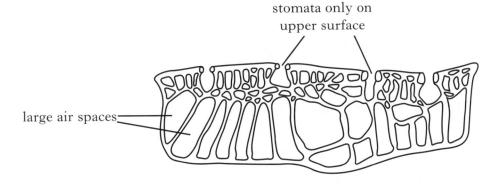

stomata only on
upper surface

large air spaces

Explain how the large air spaces allow this plant to survive in its environment.

_____

_____

_____

2

Marks

10. The Jacob-Monod hypothesis describes lactose metabolism in the bacterium *Escherichia coli*. Lactose acts as an inducer of the enzyme β-galactosidase in the bacterium. This enzyme breaks down lactose as shown.

$$\text{lactose} \xrightarrow{\text{β-galactosidase}} \text{glucose + galactose}$$

An investigation of this reaction in *E. coli* at 25 °C was carried out as described below.

- 100 cm³ of gel beads coated with *E. coli* were placed into each of seven identical funnels fitted with outlet taps.

- 100 cm³ of solution containing 2 grams of lactose was poured into each funnel.

- At each time shown in the table, the solution from one of the funnels was collected.

- The mass of lactose in each solution was measured.

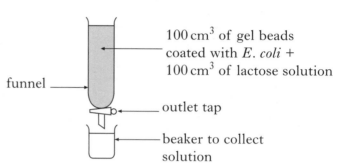

The results are shown in the table below.

Funnel	Time (minutes)	Mass of lactose in the solution collected (g)
1	0	2·00
2	10	2·00
3	20	1·48
4	30	0·92
5	40	0·40
6	50	0·12
7	60	0·04

(a) (i) Identify **one** variable, not already mentioned, that should have been controlled to ensure that the experimental procedure was valid.

_____

1

(ii) A control experiment would be needed for each funnel.

Describe such a control and explain its purpose in the investigation.

Description _____

_____

Purpose_____

_____

2

Marks

10. (continued)

(b) On the grid provided below, draw a line graph to show the mass of lactose in the solution collected against time.

Use an appropriate scale to fill most of the grid.

(Additional graph paper, if required, will be found on *Page thirty-six*.)

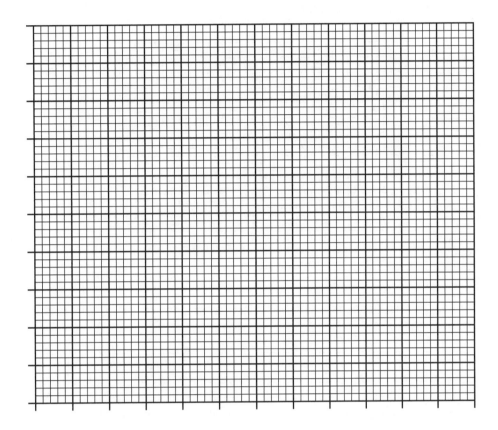

2

(c) Calculate the average mass of lactose broken down per minute in funnel 5.

Space for calculation

_____ g per minute   1

(d) Use the information given to explain why *E. coli* had not broken down any lactose in the first 10 minutes.

_____

_____

_____   2

(e) State **one** advantage to *E. coli* of controlling lactose metabolism as described by the Jacob-Monod hypothesis.

_____

1

Marks

11. (a) The graph below shows the change in the dry mass of an annual plant as it grows from a seed over an eight week period.

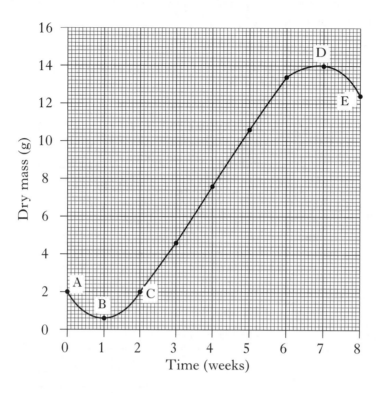

(i) Tick (✓) **two** boxes to identify periods when the rate of growth was the same.

☐ ☐ ☐ ☐ ☐ ☐ ☐ ☐

0–1 weeks   1–2 weeks   2–3 weeks   3–4 weeks   4–5 weeks   5–6 weeks   6–7 weeks   7–8 weeks

1

(ii) Which letter indicates the beginning of germination?

Letter _____

1

(iii) Which process accounts for the rise in dry mass between B and C?

_____

1

(iv) Suggest a reason for the decrease in dry mass between D and E.

_____

1

(b) Apart from the increase in mass, state **one** other way in which the growth of an annual plant could be measured.

_____

1

(c) Name the region of a shoot or root tip of an annual plant in which cell division occurs.

_____

1

DO NOT
WRITE IN
THIS
MARGIN

Marks

12. Phenylalanine and tyrosine are amino acids produced from the digestion of protein in the human diet. Once absorbed, they are involved in the metabolic pathway shown below.

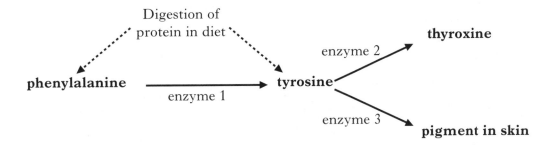

The condition phenylketonuria (PKU) can be caused by the absence of enzyme 1.

(a) Describe what leads to the absence of enzyme 1 in this condition.

_____

_____   1

(b) Explain why individuals with PKU still develop some pigment in their skin.

_____

_____   1

(c) State the role of thyroxine in the human body.

_____

_____   1

[Turn over

Marks

13. The diagrams show three barley seedlings which were grown in culture solutions. Solution A had all elements required for plant growth. Solutions B and C were each missing in one element required for normal plant growth. The seedlings were kept under a lamp which provided constant bright light conditions.

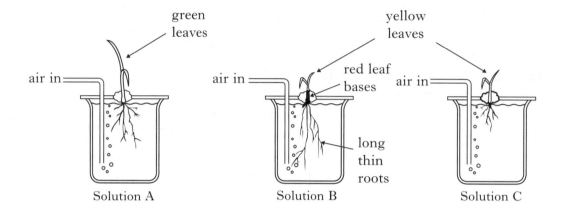

(a) Complete the table below by naming the element that was missing from culture solutions B and C and by giving a role for the element missing from solution B.

Solution	Element missing from solution	Role of element in plants
B		
C		component of chlorophyll

2

(b) In a further experiment, the seedling in solution A was grown in complete darkness for a week.

Give the term which would describe the seedling after this period and describe how the treatment would have affected its appearance.

Term _____   1

Description _____

_____   1

Marks

14. (*a*) The Colorado beetle is a pest of potato crops. In an investigation, the population of beetles in a 2000 m² potato field was estimated as described below.

A sample of the beetles from the field was collected and counted.

Each beetle was marked with a spot of paint then released back into the field.

Three days later a second sample of beetles was collected and counted.

The number of marked beetles in this second sample was noted.

The results are shown in the table below.

Number of beetles that were marked and released	Number of beetles in second sample	Number of marked beetles in second sample
500	450	5

The population of beetles can be estimated using the following formula.

$$\text{Population} = \frac{\text{number of beetles marked and released} \times \text{number of beetles in second sample}}{\text{number of marked beetles in second sample}}$$

(i) Calculate the **population density** of beetles in the field.

Space for calculation

_____ beetles per m²   **1**

(ii) The beetle population is affected by both density-dependent and density-independent factors.

Name a density-dependent and a density-independent factor that could affect the population of beetles in the field.

Density-dependent factor _____

Density-independent factor _____   **1**

(*b*) A population of a species may be monitored to gain data for use in pest control.

State **two** further reasons why a wild population may be monitored.

1 _____

2 _____   **1**

[Turn over for Section C on *Page thirty-two*

Marks

SECTION C

Both questions in this section should be attempted.

Note that each question contains a choice.

Questions 1 and 2 should be attempted on the blank pages which follow.

Supplementary sheets, if required, may be obtained from the Invigilator.

All answers must be written clearly and legibly in ink.

Labelled diagrams may be used where appropriate.

1. Answer **either** A **or** B.

   A. Write notes on plant growth and development under the following headings:

   (i)   the effects of indole acetic acid (IAA);   **6**

   (ii) the role of gibberellic acid (GA) in the germination of barley grains.   **4**

                                                                                      (10)

   OR

   B. Write notes on the following:

   (i)   endotherms and ectotherms;   **2**

   (ii) temperature regulation in mammals.   **8**

                                                                                      (10)

In question 2, ONE mark is available for coherence and ONE mark is available for relevance.

2. Answer **either** A **or** B.

   A. Give an account of the importance of isolating mechanisms, mutations and natural selection in the evolution of new species.   **(10)**

   OR

   B. Give an account of the transpiration stream and its importance to plants.   **(10)**

[END OF QUESTION PAPER]

[BLANK PAGE]

FOR OFFICIAL USE

Total for
Sections
B and C

X007/301

NATIONAL
QUALIFICATIONS
2011

WEDNESDAY, 1 JUNE
1.00 PM – 3.30 PM

BIOLOGY
HIGHER

Fill in these boxes and read what is printed below.

Full name of centre

Town

Forename(s)

Surname

Date of birth

Day	Month	Year	Scottish candidate number	Number of seat

SECTION A—Questions 1–30 (30 marks)

Instructions for completion of Section A are given on page two.

For this section of the examination you must use an **HB pencil**.

SECTIONS B AND C (100 marks)

1   (a)   All questions should be attempted.

    (b)   It should be noted that in **Section C** questions 1 and 2 each contain a choice.

2   The questions may be answered in any order but all answers are to be written in the spaces provided in this answer book, **and must be written clearly and legibly in ink**.

3   Additional space for answers will be found at the end of the book. If further space is required, supplementary sheets may be obtained from the Invigilator and should be inserted inside the **front** cover of this book.

4   The numbers of questions must be clearly inserted with any answers written in the additional space.

5   Rough work, if any should be necessary, should be written in this book and then scored through when the fair copy has been written. If further space is required a supplementary sheet for rough work may be obtained from the Invigilator.

6   Before leaving the examination room you must give this book to the Invigilator. If you do not, you may lose all the marks for this paper.

Read carefully

1   Check that the answer sheet provided is for **Biology Higher (Section A)**.

2   For this section of the examination you must use an **HB pencil**, and where necessary, an eraser.

3   Check that the answer sheet you have been given has **your name**, **date of birth**, **SCN** (Scottish Candidate Number) and **Centre Name** printed on it.

Do not change any of these details.

4   If any of this information is wrong, tell the Invigilator immediately.

5   If this information is correct, **print** your name and seat number in the boxes provided.

6   The answer to each question is **either** A, B, C or D. Decide what your answer is, then, using your pencil, put a horizontal line in the space provided (see sample question below).

7   There is **only one correct** answer to each question.

8   Any rough working should be done on the question paper or the rough working sheet, **not** on your answer sheet.

9   At the end of the examination, put the **answer sheet for Section A inside the front cover of this answer book**.

Sample Question

The apparatus used to determine the energy stored in a foodstuff is a

A   calorimeter

B   respirometer

C   klinostat

D   gas burette.

The correct answer is **A**—calorimeter. The answer **A** has been clearly marked in **pencil** with a horizontal line (see below).

Changing an answer

If you decide to change your answer, carefully erase your first answer and using your pencil fill in the answer you want. The answer below has been changed to **D**.

SECTION A

All questions in this section should be attempted.

Answers should be given on the separate answer sheet provided.

1. Equal sized pieces of potato were weighed then placed in different concentrations of sucrose.

   After 24 hours the potato pieces were removed and reweighed.

   For each potato piece the initial mass divided by the final mass was calculated.

   Which graph correctly represents the change in initial mass divided by final mass which would be expected as the concentration of sucrose increases?

   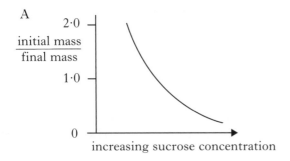

   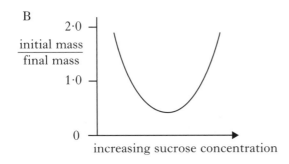

   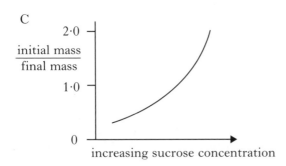

   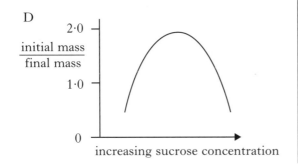

2. The graph below shows the rate of photosynthesis at two different levels of carbon dioxide concentration at 20 °C.

   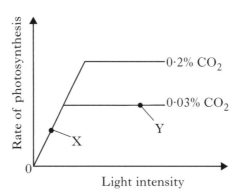

   From the evidence given, identify the factors most likely to be limiting the rate of photosynthesis at points X and Y on the graph.

	Point X	Point Y
A	Light intensity	CO_2 concentration
B	Temperature	Light intensity
C	CO_2 concentration	Temperature
D	Light intensity	Temperature

   [Turn over

3. The diagram below represents a summary of respiration in a mammalian muscle cell.

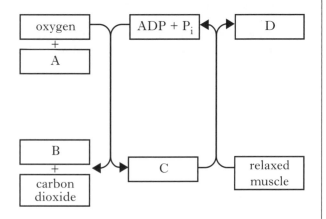

Which box represents ATP?

4. Which of the following produces water?

   A   Krebs cycle

   B   Glycolysis

   C   Photolysis

   D   Cytochrome system

5. The graph below shows changes which occur in the masses of protein, fat and carbohydrate in the body of a hibernating mammal during seven weeks without food.

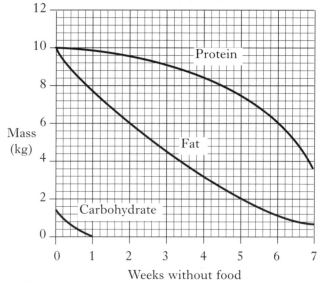

What percentage of the original mass of fat was used up between weeks 2 and 5?

   A   33%

   B   40%

   C   67%

   D   80%

6. Which of the following compounds are linked by peptide bonds to form more complex molecules?

   A   Bases

   B   Nucleic acids

   C   Nucleotides

   D   Amino acids

7. A DNA molecule consists of 4000 nucleotides, of which 20% contain the base adenine.

   How many of the nucleotides in this DNA molecule will contain guanine?

   A   800

   B   1000

   C   1200

   D   1600

8. The diagram below shows parts of an animal cell.

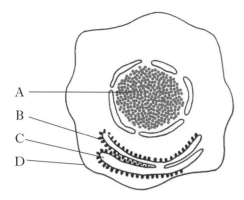

Where does synthesis of mRNA take place?

9. The function of tRNA in cell metabolism is to

   A transport amino acids to be used in synthesis

   B carry codons to the ribosomes

   C synthesise proteins

   D transcribe the DNA code.

10. Which of the following describes a cellular defence mechanism in plants?

   A Growth of sharp spines

   B Production of cellulose fibres

   C Development of low meristems

   D Secretion of sticky resin

11. Huntington's Disease is an inherited condition in humans caused by a dominant allele. A woman's father is heterozygous for the condition. Her mother is not affected by the condition.

   What is the chance of the woman being affected by the condition?

   A 1 in 1

   B 1 in 2

   C 1 in 3

   D 1 in 4

12. In guinea pigs, brown hair **B** is dominant to white hair **b** and short hair **S** is dominant to long hair **s**.

   A brown, long-haired male was crossed with a white, short-haired female. The F_1 phenotype ratio was

   1 brown, short-haired:
   1 white, short-haired:
   1 brown, long-haired:
   1 white, long-haired.

   What were the genotypes of the parents?

	Male	*Female*
A	BbSs	BbSs
B	Bbss	bbSs
C	BBss	bbSS
D	bbSs	Bbss

13. The following cross was carried out using two true-breeding strains of the fruit fly, *Drosophila*.

   Parents　straight wing　×　curly wing
   　　　　　black body　　　grey body

   F_1　　　all straight wing
   　　　　　black body

   　　　F_1 allowed to interbreed

   F_2　3 straight wing　:　1 curly wing
   　　　black body　　　　grey body

   The result would suggest that

   A crossing over has occurred between the genes

   B before isolation, F_1 females had mated with their own-type males

   C non-disjunction of chromosomes in the sex cells has taken place

   D these genes are linked.

   [Turn over

14. The diagram below shows the chromosome complement of cells during the development of abnormal human sperm.

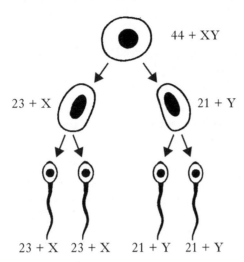

A sperm with chromosome complement 23 + X fertilises a normal haploid egg. What is the chromosome number and sex of the resulting zygote?

	Chromosome number	Sex of zygote
A	24	female
B	46	female
C	46	male
D	47	female

15. The diagram below represents the areas of interbreeding of 4 groups of birds, W, X, Y and Z.

Interbreeding takes place in the shaded areas.

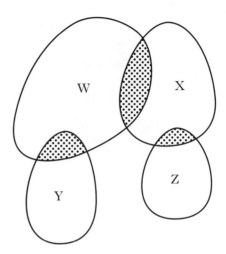

How many species are present?

A 1

B 2

C 3

D 4

16. In an investigation, peppered moths of both light and dark varieties were marked and released in three woodland areas. The numbers recaptured after 24 hours are shown in the table below.

Woodland area	Variety released	Number released	Number recaptured
1	Light	70	35
1	Dark	30	15
2	Light	450	150
2	Dark	300	150
3	Light	120	12
3	Dark	220	22

The woodland areas were graded as polluted if the percentage of dark moths recaptured was greater than the percentage of light moths recaptured.

Which of the woodland areas were graded as polluted?

A   1 and 2 only

B   2 and 3 only

C   2 only

D   1 and 3 only

17. Apparatus X shown below is used in investigations into the rate of transpiration of a leafy twig.

Apparatus Y is a control used in such investigations.

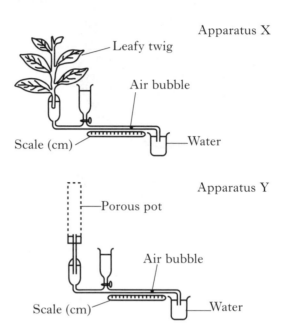

The distance travelled by the air bubble in a given time measures the rate of transpiration in the leafy twig and the rate of evaporation from the porous pot.

Which line in the table below shows how the distance travelled by the air bubble changes when apparatus X and Y are moved from light to dark with all other variables kept constant?

	Distance travelled by air bubble (cm per minute)	
	Apparatus X	Apparatus Y
A	decreases	decreases
B	decreases	unchanged
C	increases	unchanged
D	increases	increases

[Turn over

18. The diagram below shows a cross section through the stem of a hydrophyte.

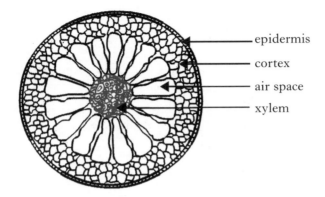

The arrangement of the xylem is of benefit to the plant because it

A   gives the stem flexibility in flowing water

B   allows uptake of water through the cortex

C   gives the stem increased support

D   allows transport of sugars to the roots.

19. The statements below relate to bird behaviour.

1   Blackbirds sing to mark their territory.

2   Arctic and common terns form large mixed breeding colonies.

3   Black grouse gather on open areas of short grass and males display to females.

4   Great skuas chase other seabirds and force them to drop their food.

Which of the above statements are related to intraspecific competition?

A   1 and 2 only

B   1 and 3 only

C   2 and 4 only

D   3 and 4 only

20. When the intensity of grazing by herbivores increases in a grassland ecosystem, diversity of plant species may increase as a result.

Which statement explains this observation?

A   Few herbivores are able to eat every plant species present.

B   Grazing stimulates growth in some plant species.

C   Vigorous plant species are eaten so less competitive species can now thrive.

D   Plant species with defences against herbivores are selected.

21. The diagram below shows a section through a woody twig.

Which label shows the position of a meristem?

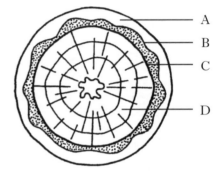

22. In the condition phenylketonuria (PKU), the human body is unable to

A   synthesise phenylalanine from tyrosine

B   secrete phenylalanine from cells

C   absorb phenylalanine into the bloodstream

D   convert phenylalanine to tyrosine.

23. The diagram below shows an experiment to investigate the role of IAA in the growth of lateral buds.

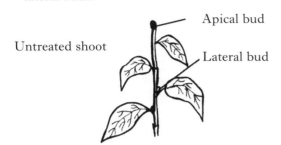

Untreated shoot

Apical bud

Lateral bud

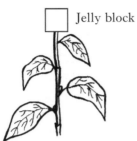

Jelly block

Apical bud removed and replaced by a jelly block

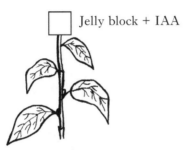

Jelly block + IAA

Apical bud removed and replaced by a jelly block containing IAA

Which line in the table correctly shows the expected growth of lateral buds in the experiment?

✓ = growth of lateral buds
✗ = no growth of lateral buds

	Untreated shoot	Apical bud removed and replaced by jelly block	Apical bud removed and replaced by a jelly block containing IAA
A	✗	✓	✗
B	✗	✗	✓
C	✓	✓	✗
D	✓	✗	✓

24. The table below shows the results of an experiment to investigate the effect of IAA on the development of roots from sections of pea stems.

Concentration of IAA (units)	Average number of roots per stem section
2	2·0
4	2·2
6	3·8
8	5·7
10	6·6

The greatest percentage increase in the average number of roots per stem section is caused by an increase in IAA concentration (units) from

A   2 to 4

B   4 to 6

C   6 to 8

D   8 to 10.

[Turn over

25. The graph below shows how female bone density changes with age.

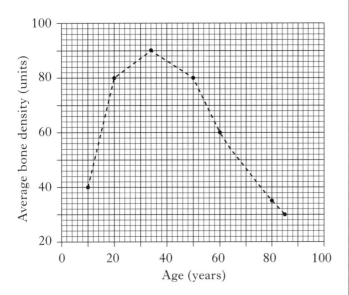

When a female's bone density falls to 60% of its maximum, there is an increased chance of bone breakage.

This occurs at

A   60 years

B   64 years

C   76 years

D   84 years.

26. The diagrams below represent the same barley seedling at 24 hours and 30 hours after germination.

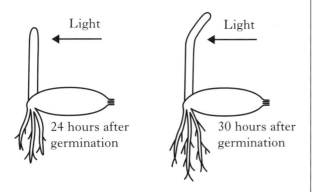

Which of the following is used to describe the growth movement observed?

A   Photoperiodism

B   Etiolation

C   Phototropism

D   Germination

27. Which line in the table below shows the critical factors for the onset of flowering in short and long day plants?

	Short day plants	Long day plants
A	length of light period	length of light period
B	length of dark period	length of dark period
C	length of light period	length of dark period
D	length of dark period	length of light period

28. An experiment was carried out to estimate the concentration of urea present in urine samples as shown in the diagram below.

The method involved adding tablets containing the enzyme urease to urine samples. Urease breaks down urea to produce ammonia.

The time taken for the ammonia produced to turn red litmus to blue was then measured.

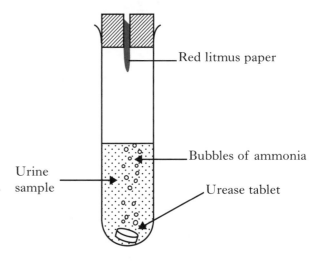

Which **two** factors would have to be kept the same throughout the investigation?

A   Size of tablet and concentration of urea

B   Concentration of urea and time taken for red litmus to turn blue

C   Size of tablet and volume of urine used

D   Volume of urine used and time taken for red litmus to turn blue

29. Which line in the table below shows density-dependent and density-independent factors?

	Density-dependent	Density-independent
A	disease and competition	flood and drought
B	fire and flood	food supply and predation
C	food supply and disease	competition and predation
D	competition and fire	flood and drought

30. Which line in the table below identifies the characteristics of a climax community?

	Characteristic of climax community		
	Biomass	Species diversity	Food webs
A	low	high	simple
B	high	low	complex
C	low	low	simple
D	high	high	complex

Candidates are reminded that the answer sheet MUST be returned INSIDE the front cover of this answer book.

[Turn over

Marks

SECTION B

All questions in this section should be attempted.

All answers must be written clearly and legibly in ink.

1. The diagram below shows *Paramecium*, a unicellular organism found in fresh water.

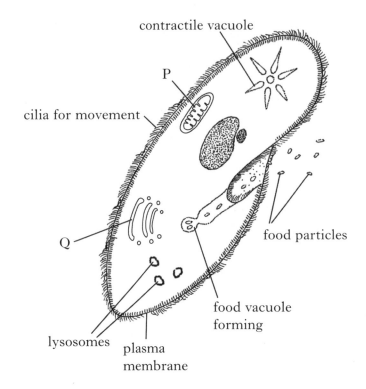

(a) Identify organelles P and Q.

   P _____

   Q _____   2

(b)   (i) Name **two** chemical components of the plasma membrane.

         1 _____

         2 _____   1

      (ii) Give a property of the plasma membrane which is related to its role in osmosis.

         _____   1

Marks

1. **(continued)**

    (*c*) *Paramecium* has contractile vacuoles that fill with excess water which has entered the organism by osmosis. These vacuoles contract to remove this water from the organism.

    The rate of contraction of the vacuoles is affected by the concentration of the solution in which the *Paramecium* is found.

    In which solution would the highest rate of contraction of the vacuoles occur?

    Underline the correct answer.

    hypertonic　　　hypotonic　　　isotonic

    1

    (*d*) *Paramecium* feeds on micro-organisms present in water.

    Use information from the diagram to describe how *Paramecium* obtains and digests food.

    _____

    _____

    _____

    2

[Turn over

Marks

2. The diagram below shows an outline of respiration in yeast cells.

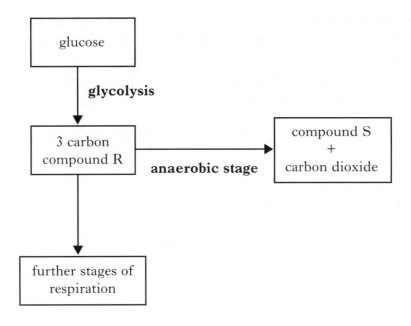

(a) State the location of glycolysis in yeast cells.

_____

1

(b) Name **one** substance, other than glucose, which must be present for glycolysis to occur.

_____

1

(c) Name compounds R and S.

R _____

1

S _____

1

(d) Explain why the further stages of respiration cannot occur in anaerobic conditions.

_____

_____

_____

1

Marks

3. The graph shows the rate of potassium ion uptake by human liver cells in different oxygen concentrations at 30 °C.

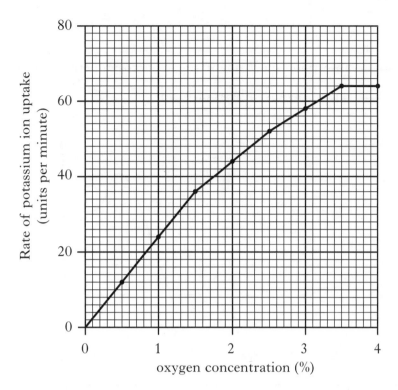

(a) When the oxygen concentration is 1%, how many units of potassium would a cell take up in one hour?

Space for calculation

_____ units per hour   **1**

(b) Suggest a reason why the graph levels off at oxygen concentrations above 3·5%.

_____

_____   **1**

(c) When the experiment was repeated at 20 °C, the potassium ion uptake decreased. Explain this observation.

_____

_____

_____

_____   **2**

Marks

4. (a) The diagram below shows the absorption spectrum of a single photosynthetic pigment from a plant and the rate of photosynthesis of the plant in different colours of light.

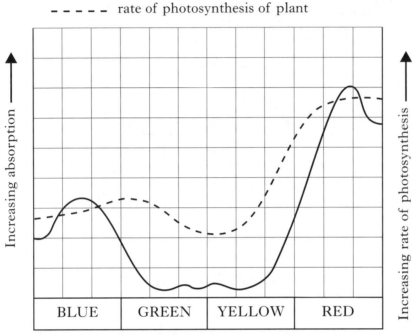

Key

———— absorption spectrum of single photosynthetic pigment

- - - - rate of photosynthesis of plant

Colour of light

(i) Leaves of this plant contain more than one photosynthetic pigment.

Use evidence from the graph to justify this statement.

_____

_____

_____ 1

(ii) Name a technique used to separate mixtures of photosynthetic pigments.

_____ 1

Marks

4. (continued)

(b) *Spirogyra* is a photosynthetic green alga which grows as a long strand of cells. A strand of *Spirogyra* was placed into water containing aerobic bacteria. Different parts of the strand were exposed to different colours of light. After a period of time, the bacteria had moved into the positions shown in the diagram below.

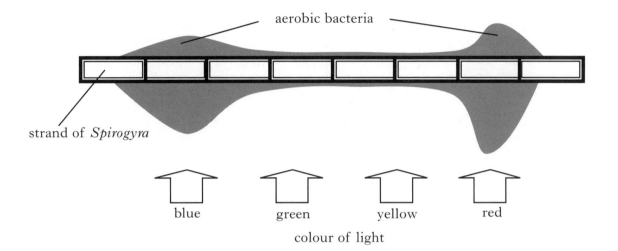

Explain the distribution of aerobic bacteria shown in the diagram.

_____

_____

_____

_____   2

[Turn over

Marks

5. (a) Eye colour in fruit flies is sex-linked.

Red eye colour **R** is dominant to white eye colour **r**.

A heterozygous red-eyed female fly was crossed with a white-eyed male.

(i) Complete the grid by adding the genotypes of

1 the male and female gametes;   1

2 the possible offspring.   1

	Female gametes	
Male gametes		

(ii) Tick (✓) the box(es) to show all the expected phenotypes of the offspring from this cross.

red-eyed female ☐   white-eyed female ☐

red-eyed male ☐   white-eyed male ☐   1

(iii) Explain why the actual phenotype **ratio** obtained from this cross could differ from the expected.

_____

_____   1

Marks

5.   (continued)

(b)   Genes K, L, M and N are located on the same chromosome in fruit flies.

The recombination frequencies of pairs of these genes are given in the table.

Genes	Recombination frequency (%)
K and L	18
N and L	25
M and N	17
L and M	8
K and N	7

Complete the diagram below to show the relative positions of genes L, M and N on the chromosome.

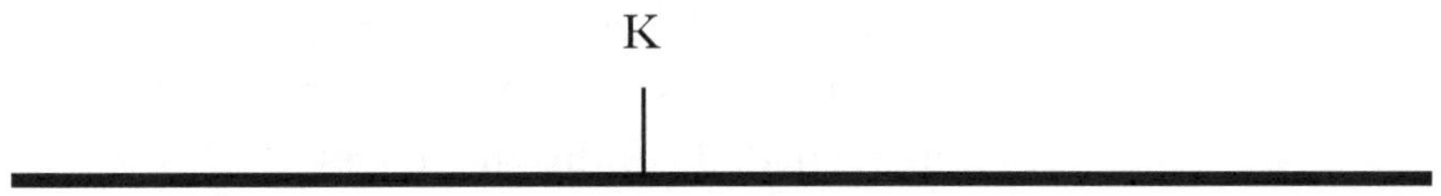

K

1

[Turn over

6. The compensation point is the light intensity at which a plant's carbon dioxide uptake by photosynthesis is equal to its carbon dioxide output from respiration.

Marks

In some plant species, compensation point can be reduced when the plant is moved from bright light to shaded conditions.

Graph 1 shows how the compensation points of three species of plant changed over a 25 day period after they were moved from bright light into shaded conditions.

Graph 1

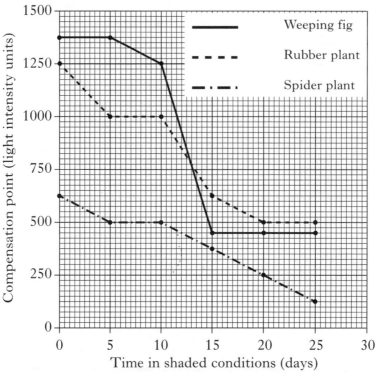

(*a*) (i) Use values from **Graph 1** to describe the changes in compensation point of the weeping fig over the 25 day period.

_____

_____

_____ 2

(ii) Calculate the percentage decrease in compensation point of the rubber plant over the 25 day period.

Space for calculation

_____ % 1

(iii) Predict the compensation point of the spider plant at **28 days**.

_____ light intensity units 1

(iv) Use evidence from the graph to explain why the rubber plant could not grow successfully in a constant light intensity of 400 light intensity units.

_____

_____ 2

Marks

6. (continued)

(b) After 10 days in shaded conditions, a plant of one species was placed into different light intensities and its carbon dioxide output and uptake were measured. This was repeated with another plant of the **same** species which had been in the shade for 20 days.

The results are shown in **Graph 2**.

Graph 2

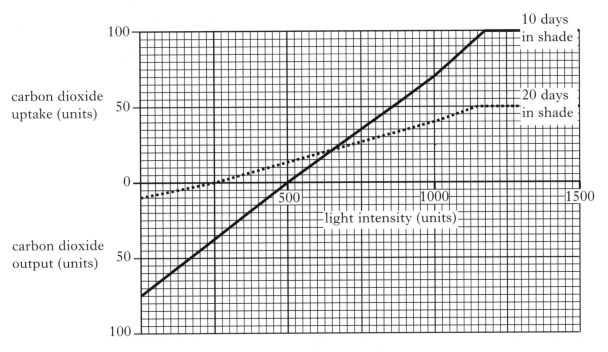

(i) Use all the data to identify the plant species referred to in **Graph 2**.

Tick (✓) the correct box and give a reason for your choice.

weeping fig ☐   rubber plant ☐   spider plant ☐

Reason

_____

_____   1

(ii) From **Graph 2**, calculate how many times greater the carbon dioxide uptake of this plant was at 1000 units of light intensity after 10 days in shaded conditions compared with after 20 days in shaded conditions.

Space for calculation

_____ times   1

Marks

7. The table shows the base sequences of some mRNA codons and the amino acids for which they code.

mRNA codon			Amino acid
first base	second base	third base	
A	G	G	arginine
		C	serine
	A	A	lysine
		U	asparagine
	C	A	threonine
		C	threonine
	U	G	methionine
		U	isoleucine
C	G	A	arginine
		C	arginine
	A	G	glutamine
		U	histidine
	C	G	proline
		C	proline
	U	A	leucine
		U	leucine

(a) (i) State the mRNA codon for methionine.

$\underline{\qquad\qquad AUG \qquad\qquad}$ 1

(ii) Use information from the table to identify the common feature of all mRNA codons which code for the amino acid arginine.

$\underline{\qquad\qquad\qquad\qquad\qquad\qquad\qquad\qquad}$ 1

(b) Complete the diagram below by naming the two amino acids corresponding to the bases on the strand of DNA shown.

Bases on strand of DNA

T A A G T C

Corresponding amino acids

1

Marks

8. Mutation rate can be increased artificially using chemical agents.

(*a*) Give **another** example of a mutagenic agent.

_____   1

(*b*) The table below shows the bases on part of a strand of DNA and the effects on the bases of four different gene mutations.

Original DNA strand	Gene mutation	Mutated DNA strands
A T C G C T A	1	A T C G G C T A
	2	A T C C T A
	3	A T C G C A A
	4	A T G C C T A

(i) Name the gene mutations which have caused the effects shown in the mutated strands.

gene mutation 1 _insertion_

gene mutation 2 _deletion_

gene mutation 3 _substitution_

gene mutation 4 _inversion_   2

(ii) Use numbers from the table to identify the **two** gene mutations that would result in the greatest changes to the structure of the protein coded for by the original DNA strand.

Explain how these mutations would lead to major changes in the structure of the protein.

Gene mutation numbers __1__ and __2__ .   1

Explanation _they are frameshift mutations –_
everything after mutation will be
read out of from so therfore   1
every AA incorrect

[Turn over

Marks

9. (a) The table shows behavioural adaptations of lions for obtaining food.

   (i) Complete the table below by explaining how each adaptation is beneficial for obtaining food.

Behavioural adaptation	Benefit for obtaining food
Cooperative hunting	
Territorial behaviour	

2

   (ii) These behavioural adaptations ensure that lions can forage economically.

   Explain what is meant by this statement in terms of energy gained and lost.

   _____

   _____

   _____   1

   (iii) Lions hunt wildebeest, which live in large herds.

   Explain how living in large herds benefits the wildebeest in terms of predation by lions.

   _____

   _____

   _____   1

Marks

9. **(continued)**

   (*b*) If a snail is disturbed, it withdraws into its shell and re-emerges a few minutes later.

   (i) Name the type of behaviour shown by the withdrawal response.

   _____   1

   (ii) What is the advantage to a snail of withdrawing into its shell?

   _____

   _____   1

[Turn over

10. Gibberellic acid (GA) is needed to break dormancy of rice grains allowing them to germinate.

An experiment was carried out to investigate the effects of GA on the germination of rice grains.

$30\,cm^3$ of different concentrations of GA solution was placed into separate beakers. 50 rice grains were added to each beaker. Each beaker was then covered with plastic film.

After 12 hours, the grains were removed from the solutions and evenly spaced in separate dishes on filter paper soaked with $20\,cm^3$ of water.

The dishes were covered and kept in the dark for 10 days and the number of germinated grains in each dish was counted.

A second batch of grains was treated in the same way but these were left in the GA solutions for 36 hours.

The results are shown in the table.

Concentration of GA solution (mg per litre)	Number of rice grains germinated	
	After 12 hours in GA solution	After 36 hours in GA solution
0	5	6
5	7	14
10	16	31
20	23	35
30	28	41
60	31	43

(a) Identify **one** variable, not already described, that should be kept constant.

_____ 1

(b) (i) Explain how the solution with 0 mg per litre GA acts as a control in this experiment.

_____

_____ 1

(ii) Suggest why some germination occurs in the control.

_____ 1

(c) Identify a feature of the experimental procedure which ensured the reliability of the results.

_____ 1

Marks

10. (continued)

(*d*) Predict how the concentration of GA in the beakers would have been affected if they had not been covered with plastic film.

Underline the correct answer and give a reason for your choice.

increased   **decreased**   **stayed the same**

Reason _____

_____   1

(*e*) Calculate the difference in **percentage** germination between the grains kept in the 5 mg GA per litre solution for 12 hours and those kept in the 30 mg GA per litre solution for 12 hours.

Space for calculation

_____ %   1

(*f*) On the grid below, draw a line graph to show the number of grains germinated after 36 hours in the different concentration of GA solution.

(Additional graph paper, if required, will be found on *Page forty*.)

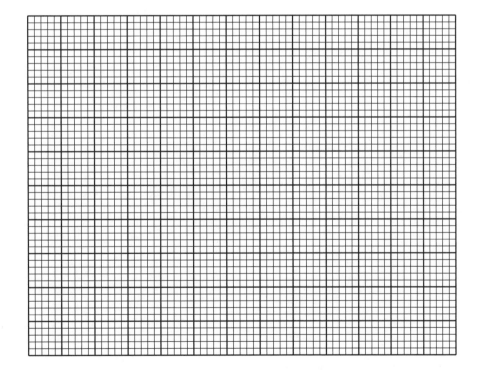

2

(*g*) Give **two** conclusions which can be drawn from the results in the **table**.

1 _____

2 _____   2

DO NOT WRITE IN THIS MARGIN

Marks

10. (continued)

(*h*) GA induces the release of amylase in the germinating grains of plants such as rice and barley.

Name the site within the grains which produces amylase.

____ **1**

Marks

11. The graph below shows how the body length of a locust changes over time.

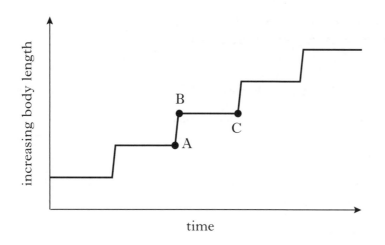

(*a*) Explain the growth pattern between points A and B and between points B and C shown on the graph.

A and B _____

_____ 1

B and C _____

_____ 1

(*b*) The diagram shows information about hormones involved in growth and development in humans.

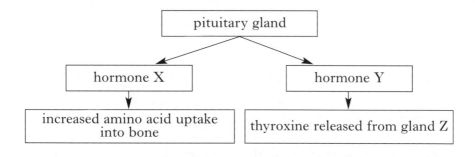

(i) Name hormones X and Y.

X _____ 1

Y _____ 1

(ii) Name gland Z.

_____ 1

(iii) Describe the role of thyroxine in growth and development.

_____

_____ 1

Marks

12. (*a*)   In the control of lactose metabolism in *Escherichia coli* (*E. coli*), lactose acts as an inducer of the enzyme β-galactosidase.

The graph shows changes in concentrations of lactose and β-galactosidase after lactose was added to an *E. coli* culture growing in a container.

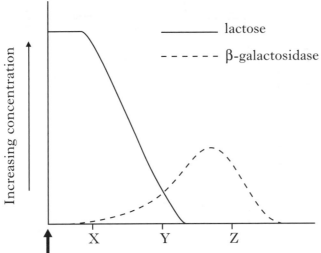

lactose
added   Time after lactose added to the *E. coli* culture

(i)   Describe how the graph supports the statement that β-galactosidase breaks down lactose.

_____

_____   **1**

(ii)   The statements in the table refer to times X, Y and Z on the graph.

Complete the table by writing **true** or **false** in each of the spaces provided.

Statement	True or False
At time X the lactose is bound to the repressor	
At time Y the lactose is bound to the operator	
At time Z the repressor is bound to the operator	

2

Marks

12. **(continued)**

(b) Complete the following sentences by <u>underlining</u> one of the alternatives in each pair.

Regeneration involves development of cells with specialised functions

from $\begin{Bmatrix} \text{differentiated} \\ \text{undifferentiated} \end{Bmatrix}$ cells through the switching on or off of

particular $\begin{Bmatrix} \text{hormones} \\ \text{genes} \end{Bmatrix}$.

Mammals have $\begin{Bmatrix} \text{limited} \\ \text{extensive} \end{Bmatrix}$ powers of regeneration.

2

[Turn over

Marks

13. The grid contains the names of substances that can influence growth and development in plants and animals.

A	B	C	D
calcium	nitrogen	iron	phosphorus
E	**F**	**G**	**H**
vitamin D	magnesium	lead	potassium

Use **letters from the grid** to answer the following questions.

Letters can be used once, more than once or not at all.

Each box should be completed using **one** letter only.

(a) Complete the table below.

Role in growth and development	Letter(s)	
Important in membrane transport		■
Present in chlorophyll		
Present in nucleic acids		
Needed for blood clotting		■

4

(b) Complete the sentence.

Deficiency of ☐ leads to rickets as a result of

poor ☐ absorption in the intestine.

1

Marks

14. The list below shows conditions which must be maintained within tolerable limits in the human body.

List
A   blood glucose concentration
B   blood water concentration
C   body temperature

(a) Use **all** the letters from the list to complete the table below to show where each condition is monitored.

Hypothalamus	Pancreas

1

(b) The liver contains a reservoir of stored carbohydrate.

Name **two** hormones which can cause the breakdown of this carbohydrate to increase the concentration of glucose in the blood.

1 _____

2 _____

1

(c) An increase in blood water concentration causes a reduction in the level of ADH in the bloodstream.

Describe the effect of this reduction on the kidney tubules.

_____

_____

1

(d) (i) When body temperature falls below normal, the blood vessels in the skin respond.

State how the blood vessels in the skin respond and explain how this helps return body temperature to normal.

Blood vessel response _____   1

Explanation _____

_____   1

(ii) What term is used to describe animals which derive most of their body heat from their own metabolism?

_____   1

Marks

SECTION C

Both questions in this section should be attempted.

Note that each question contains a choice.

Questions 1 and 2 should be attempted on the blank pages which follow.

Supplementary sheets, if required, may be obtained from the Invigilator.

All answers must be written clearly and legibly in ink.

Labelled diagrams may be used where appropriate.

1. Answer **either** A **or** B.

   A. Write notes on maintaining a water balance under the following headings:

   (i) osmoregulation in **salt water** bony fish;   6

   (ii) water conservation in the desert rat.   4

          (10)

   OR

   B. Write notes on meiosis under the following headings:

   (i) first and second meiotic divisions;   7

   (ii) its role in the production of new phenotypes.   3

          (10)

In question 2, ONE mark is available for coherence and ONE mark is available for relevance.

2. Answer **either** A **or** B.

   A. Give an account of carbon fixation in photosynthesis and its importance to plants.   (10)

   OR

   B. Give an account of the production of new viruses after the invasion of cells and the role of lymphocytes in cellular defence.   (10)

[END OF QUESTION PAPER]

SPACE FOR ANSWERS

SPACE FOR ANSWERS

Page thirty-six

SPACE FOR ANSWERS

SPACE FOR ANSWERS

SPACE FOR ANSWERS

SPACE FOR ANSWERS

SPACE FOR ANSWERS

ADDITIONAL GRAPH PAPER FOR QUESTION 10(*f*)

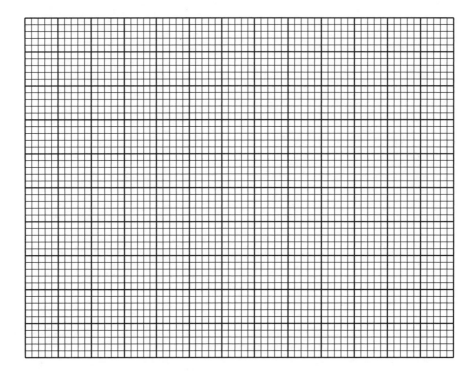

SPACE FOR ANSWERS

[BLANK PAGE]

FOR OFFICIAL USE

Total for
Sections
B and C

X007/12/02

NATIONAL
QUALIFICATIONS
2012

WEDNESDAY, 23 MAY
1.00 PM – 3.30 PM

BIOLOGY
HIGHER

Fill in these boxes and read what is printed below.

Full name of centre

Town

Forename(s)

Surname

Date of birth

Day	Month	Year	Scottish candidate number	Number of seat

SECTION A—Questions 1—30 (30 Marks)

Instructions for completion of Section A are given on *Page two*.

For this section of the examination you must use an **HB pencil**.

SECTIONS B AND C (100 Marks)

1 (a) All questions should be attempted.

   (b) It should be noted that in **Section C** questions 1 and 2 each contain a choice.

2 The questions may be answered in any order but all answers are to be written in the spaces provided in this answer book, **and must be written clearly and legibly in ink**.

3 Additional space for answers will be found at the end of the book. If further space is required, supplementary sheets may be obtained from the Invigilator and should be inserted inside the **front** cover of this book.

4 The numbers of questions must be clearly inserted with any answers written in the additional space.

5 Rough work, if any should be necessary, should be written in this book and then scored through when the fair copy has been written. If further space is required, a supplementary sheet for rough work may be obtained from the Invigilator.

6 Before leaving the examination room you must give this book to the Invigilator. If you do not, you may lose all the marks for this paper.

Read carefully

1   Check that the answer sheet provided is for **Biology Higher (Section A)**.

2   For this section of the examination you must use an **HB pencil**, and where necessary, an eraser.

3   Check that the answer sheet you have been given has **your name**, **date of birth**, **SCN** (Scottish Candidate Number) and **Centre Name** printed on it.

      Do not change any of these details.

4   If any of this information is wrong, tell the Invigilator immediately.

5   If this information is correct, **print** your name and seat number in the boxes provided.

6   The answer to each question is **either** A, B, C or D. Decide what your answer is, then, using your pencil, put a horizontal line in the space provided (see sample question below).

7   There is **only one correct** answer to each question.

8   Any rough working should be done on the question paper or the rough working sheet, **not** on your answer sheet.

9   At the end of the examination, put the **answer sheet for Section A inside the front cover of this answer book**.

Sample Question

The apparatus used to determine the energy stored in a foodstuff is a

A   calorimeter

B   respirometer

C   klinostat

D   gas burette.

The correct answer is **A**—calorimeter. The answer **A** has been clearly marked in **pencil** with a horizontal line (see below).

Changing an answer

If you decide to change your answer, carefully erase your first answer and using your pencil fill in the answer you want. The answer below has been changed to **D**.

SECTION A

All questions in this section should be attempted.

Answers should be given on the separate answer sheet provided.

1. The diagram below shows the arrangement of molecules in part of a cell membrane.

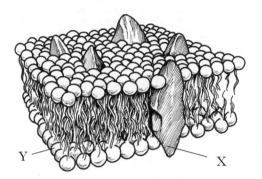

   What types of molecule are represented by X and Y?

	X	Y
A	Phospholipid	Protein
B	Protein	Phospholipid
C	Protein	Carbohydrate
D	Carbohydrate	Protein

2. The experiment below was set up to demonstrate osmosis.

   Visking tubing is selectively permeable.

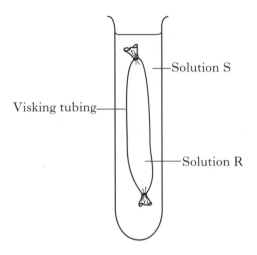

   The following results were obtained.

   Initial mass of Visking tubing
   + contents   = 10·0 g

   Mass of Visking tubing + contents
   after experiment   = 8·2 g

   The results shown above could be obtained when

   A   R is a 5% salt solution and S is a 10% salt solution

   B   R is a 10% salt solution and S is a 5% salt solution

   C   R is a 10% salt solution and S is water

   D   R is a 5% salt solution and S is water.

   [Turn over

3. The diagram below refers to the plasma membrane of an animal cell.

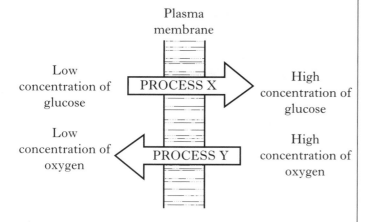

Identify the two processes X and Y.

	X	Y
A	active transport	diffusion
B	diffusion	active transport
C	respiration	diffusion
D	active transport	respiration

4. The following absorption spectra were obtained from four different plant extracts. Black areas indicate light which has been absorbed by the extracts.

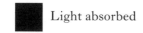

Which extract contains chlorophyll?

5. The graph below shows changes in the mass of chlorophyll and rate of photosynthesis in leaves during a 10 day period in autumn.

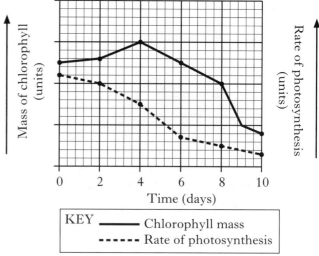

Chlorophyll content of leaves can limit the rate of photosynthesis.

During which period do the results **not** support this statement?

A   0–4 days

B   4–8 days

C   8–9 days

D   9–10 days

6. The processes in the list below occur in living cells.

1 NADP acts as a hydrogen acceptor.

2 ATP is synthesised.

3 Oxygen acts as a hydrogen acceptor.

4 Carbon dioxide enters a cycle of reactions.

Which line of the table below matches each process with the set of reactions in which it occurs?

	Set of reactions		
	Respiration only	Photosynthesis only	Respiration and photosynthesis
A	2	1 and 4	3
B	3	1 and 4	2
C	2	4	1 and 3
D	3	4	1 and 2

7. The statements in the list below refer to respiration.

   1   Carbon dioxide is released.

   2   Occurs during aerobic respiration.

   3   The end product is pyruvic acid.

   4   The end product is lactic acid.

   Which statements describe glycolysis?

   A   1 and 4

   B   1 and 3

   C   2 and 3

   D   2 and 4

8. The graph below shows changes in food stores in a human body during four weeks without food.

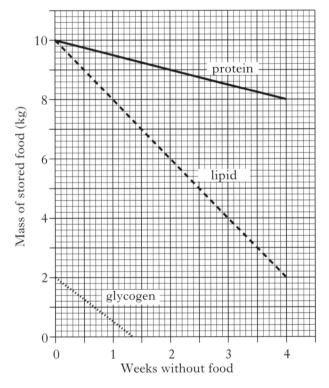

   Which of the following conclusions can be drawn from the graph?

   A   Each food store decreases at the same rate during week one.

   B   Between weeks three and four the body gains most energy from protein.

   C   The lipid food store decreases at a faster rate than the other food stores during week one.

   D   Between weeks one and four, the body only gains energy from lipid and protein.

9. A fragment of DNA was found to consist of 72 nucleotide base pairs. What is the total number of deoxyribose sugars in this fragment?

   A   24

   B   36

   C   72

   D   144

10. Insulin synthesised in a pancreatic cell is secreted. Its route from synthesis to secretion includes

   A   Golgi apparatus → endoplasmic reticulum → ribosome

   B   ribosome → Golgi apparatus → endoplasmic reticulum

   C   endoplasmic reticulum → ribosome → Golgi apparatus

   D   ribosome→ endoplasmic reticulum → Golgi apparatus.

11. The following diagram shows a pair of homologous chromosomes and the positions of 4 genes.

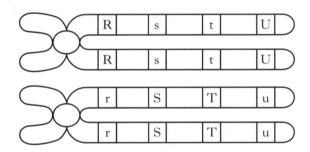

   Between which of the following alleles would chiasma formation occur least often?

   A   r and t

   B   r and U

   C   r and s

   D   s and u

   [Turn over

12. White eye colour in *Drosophila* is caused by a recessive sex-linked allele. The dominant allele is for red eyes.

    What result would be obtained from a cross between a white-eyed female and a red-eyed male?

    A   All white-eyed flies

    B   All red-eyed flies

    C   Equal numbers of white-eyed and red-eyed flies.

    D   Three times as many red-eyed flies as white-eyed flies

13. Which of the following is true of polyploid plants?

    A   They have reduced yield and the diploid chromosome number.

    B   They have increased yield and the diploid chromosome number.

    C   They have reduced yield and sets of chromosomes greater than diploid.

    D   They have increased yield and sets of chromosomes greater than diploid.

14. Which of the following gene mutations alters all the amino acids in the protein being coded for, from the position of the mutation?

    A   Deletion and insertion

    B   Deletion and substitution

    C   Inversion and substitution

    D   Insertion and inversion

15. The following steps are involved in the process of genetic engineering.

    1   Insertion of a plasmid into a bacterial host cell.

    2   Use of an enzyme to cut out the desired gene from a chromosome.

    3   Insertion of the desired gene into the bacterial plasmid.

    4   Use of an enzyme to open a bacterial plasmid.

    What is the correct sequence of these steps?

    A   4   1   2   3

    B   2   4   3   1

    C   4   3   1   2

    D   2   3   4   1

16. Which of the following is the function of cellulase in the process of somatic fusion in plants?

    A   Conversion of cells to protoplasts

    B   Isolation of cells from the parent plants

    C   Fusion of protoplasts from different plants

    D   Callus formation from hybrid protoplasts

17. The drinking rate and concentrations of sodium and chloride ions in blood were measured over a six hour period after a salmon was transferred from freshwater to sea water. The results are shown in the graph below.

Key

.... Drinking rate
– – – – Sodium ions
———— Chloride ions

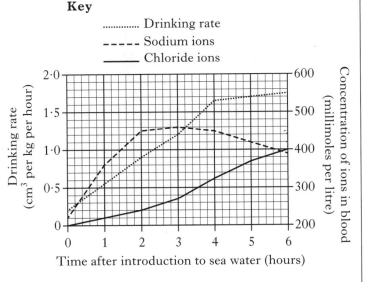

Which line in the table correctly shows the results after three hours?

	Drinking rate (cm³ per kg per hour)	Sodium ion concentration (millimoles per litre)	Chloride ion concentration (millimoles per litre)
A	1·4	270	460
B	1·2	460	270
C	1·2	270	460
D	1·4	460	270

18. Under which of the following conditions is the rate of transpiration in a plant likely to be the highest?

	Wind speed	Air temperature	Air humidity
A	high	high	high
B	high	high	low
C	high	low	low
D	low	high	high

19. Which line in the table below shows features likely to be found in a plant and in a small mammal **both** adapted to life in hot desert conditions?

	Plant	Small mammal
A	reduced root system	large number of sweat glands
B	rolled leaves	large number of glomeruli
C	small number of stomata	nocturnal habit
D	succulent tissues	short kidney tubules

20. An investigation was set up to demonstrate the response of flatworms to the presence of food. A piece of liver and a glass bead were placed in a dish. 15 flatworms were then scattered randomly into the dish as shown in the diagram below.

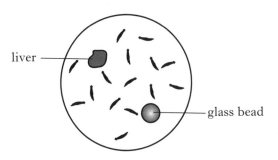

The purpose of the glass bead is to show that flatworms

A   use cooperative foraging behaviour

B   respond differently to food compared to other objects

C   move randomly in search of food

D   move towards any large object in the search for food.

[Turn over

21. The graph below shows the growth, in length, of a human fetus during pregnancy.

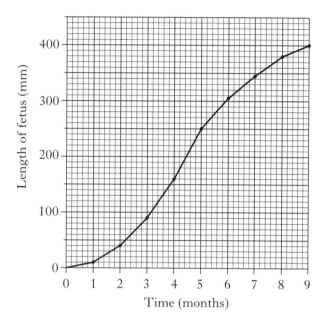

What is the percentage increase in length of the fetus during the final 4 months of pregnancy?

A　33·3

B　60·0

C　62·5

D　150·0

22. The diagram below shows a section of a woody twig.

Identify the position of a meristem.

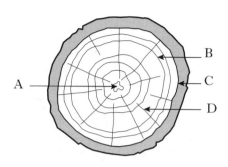

23. In which of the following processes does gibberellic acid (GA) have a role during the growth and development of plants?

A　Breaking dormancy

B　Root formation in cuttings

C　Leaf abscission

D　Apical dominance

24. The table below contains descriptions of terms used to illustrate the control of lactose metabolism in the bacterium *Esherichia coli*.

Which line in the table contains terms which correctly match the descriptions given?

	Description			
	Produces lactose digesting enzyme	*Acts as the inducer*	*Produces repressor molecule*	*Switches on structural gene*
A	regulator gene	repressor molecule	structural gene	lactose
B	structural gene	repressor molecule	regulator gene	lactose
C	regulator gene	lactose	structural gene	operator
D	structural gene	lactose	regulator gene	operator

25. An investigation into the influence of different concentrations of IAA on the development of certain plant organs was carried out. The growth-inhibiting or growth-promoting effects are shown below.

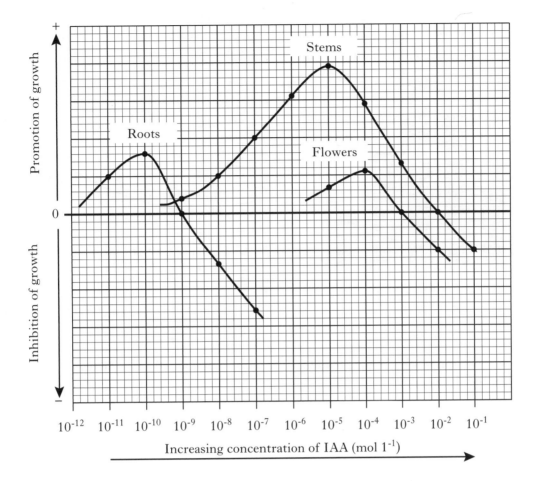

The graph shows that an IAA concentration of

A 10^{-3} mol 1^{-1} promotes flower and stem growth

B 10^{-5} mol 1^{-1} promotes stem and flower growth

C 10^{-7} mol 1^{-1} promotes root and stem growth

D 10^{-9} mol 1^{-1} inhibits stem growth and promotes root growth.

[Turn over

26. The bar chart shows the units of vitamin D provided by 100 g of various foods and the graph shows the number of units required daily by humans of different ages.

Bar chart   **Graph**

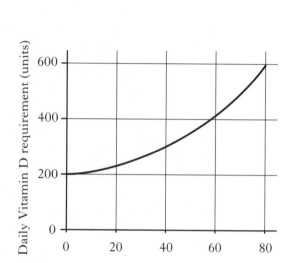

At what age would eating 100 g of tuna fish and 100 g of margarine exactly provide the number of units of vitamin D required in one day?

A   0 (birth)

B   40

C   65

D   70

27. The list below shows effects of various drugs on fetal development.

1   Reduced growth

2   Limb deformation

3   Reduced mental development.

Which effects are associated with the intake of nicotine during pregnancy in humans?

A   1 only

B   1 and 2 only

C   1 and 3 only

D   1, 2 and 3

28. Which of the following best defines etiolation?

A   The inhibition of development of lateral buds

B   The result of a magnesium deficiency in seedlings

C   The growth of a stem towards directional light

D   The effect on seedlings of being grown in the dark

29. An effect of a high concentration of antidiuretic hormone (ADH) on the kidney is to

A   increase tubule permeability which increases water reabsorption

B   decrease tubule permeability which prevents excessive water loss

C   increase glomerular filtration rate which increases urine production

D   decrease glomerular filtration rate which reduces urine production.

30. The graph below shows the changes in the populations of red and grey squirrels in an area of woodland over a 10 year period.

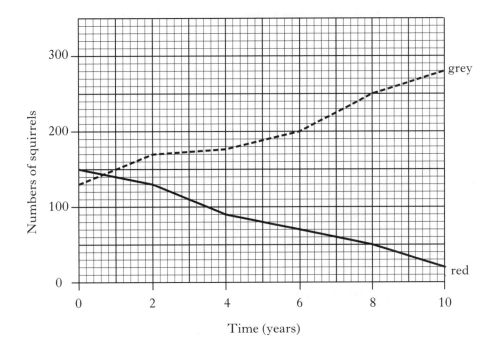

From the graph the following conclusions were suggested.

1   The grey squirrel population increases by 150% over the ten year period.

2   The red squirrel numbers decreased from 150 to 20 over the ten year period.

3   After eight years the grey squirrel population was five times greater than the red.

Which of the conclusions are correct?

A   1 and 2 only

B   1 and 3 only

C   2 and 3 only

D   1, 2 and 3

Candidates are reminded that the answer sheet MUST be returned INSIDE the front cover of this answer book.

[Turn over

SECTION B

All questions in this section should be attempted.

All answers must be written clearly and legibly in ink.

Marks

1. (*a*) The diagrams show a normal chloroplast and one from a plant treated with a weedkiller.

Normal chloroplast   Chloroplast from treated plant

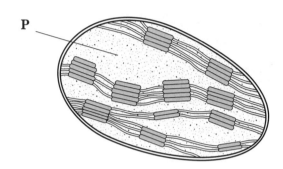 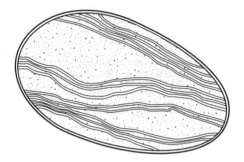

(i) Name area **P**.

_____   **1**

(ii) Describe how the structure of the chloroplast from the treated plant has been affected by the weedkiller.

_____

_____   **1**

(iii) The production of two substances required for the carbon fixation stage (Calvin cycle) was significantly decreased in the treated plant.

Name these **two** substances.

1 _____

2 _____   **2**

1. **(continued)**

Marks

(b) In an investigation into the carbon fixation stage of photosynthesis, algal cells were kept in a constant light intensity at 20 °C. The concentration of ribulose bisphosphate (RuBP) and glycerate phosphate (GP) in the cells was measured through the investigation.

The concentration of carbon dioxide available was changed from 1% to 0·003% as shown on the graph.

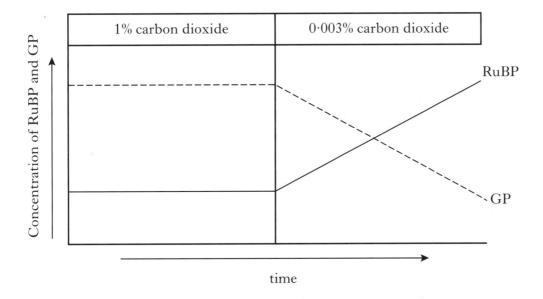

Explain the increase in RuBP concentration shown on the graph after the carbon dioxide concentration was reduced from 1% to 0·003%.

_____

_____

_____

_____   2

[Turn over

Marks

2. The diagram shows a stage in the synthesis of a protein.

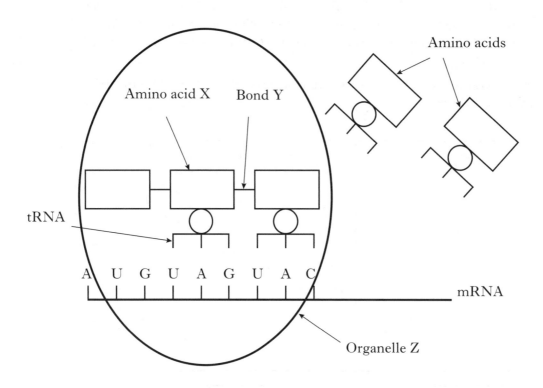

(a) Complete the diagram below by adding the appropriate letters to show the sequence of nine bases on the DNA strand from which the mRNA strand shown has been transcribed.

DNA strand   1

(b) Name organelle Z.

_____ ribgenre _____   1

(c) Give the anticodon which would be found on the tRNA carrying amino acid X in the diagram.

_____ A U C _____   1

(d) Name bond Y.

_____ peptide _____   1

Marks

3. An investigation was carried out to study the effects of the concentration of sucrose solutions on pieces of tulip stem 45 mm in length. The pieces were placed in different concentrations of sucrose solution and measured after two hours of immersion.

   The results are shown in the table below.

Sucrose concentration (moles per litre)	Length after 2 hours (mm)
0·2	50
0·3	48
0·4	46
0·5	44
0·6	42
0·7	42
0·8	42

   (a) Explain the effect of the 0·2 moles per litre sucrose solution on the length of the pieces of the tulip stem.

   _____

   _____

   _____   1

   (b) Use information from the table to predict the concentration of a sucrose solution isotonic to the cells in the tulip stem.

   _____ moles per litre   1

   (c) Give the term which would be used to describe the cells in the tulip stem after immersion in a solution with a sucrose concentration of 0·7 moles per litre.

   _____   1

   [Turn over

4. The diagram shows apparatus used in an investigation of aerobic respiration in snails.

Marks

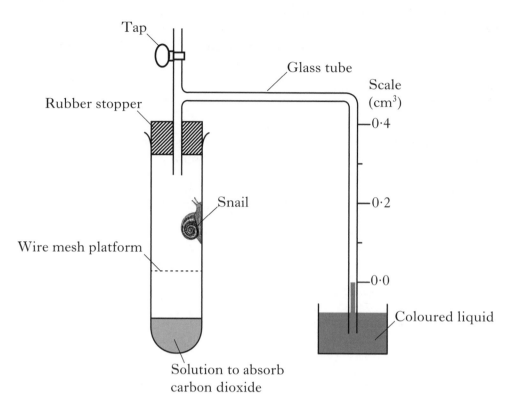

The tap was kept open to the air for 15 minutes, and to start the experiment the tap was closed and the reading on the scale recorded. Every 2 minutes for 10 minutes the reading on the scale was again recorded and the results shown in the table below. The apparatus was kept at 20 °C throughout.

Time after tap closed (minutes)	Reading on scale (cm³)
0	0·00
2	0·04
4	0·08
6	0·12
8	0·16
10	0·20

(a) State why the apparatus was left for 15 minutes with the tap open before readings were taken.

_____ 1

(b) Describe a suitable control for this investigation.

_____

_____ 1

4. (continued)

Marks

(c) To increase the reliability of results, the experiment was repeated several times. Identify **one** variable, not already mentioned, that would have to be kept the same each time to ensure that the procedure was valid.

_____

1

(d) On the grid below, draw a line graph to show the reading on the scale against time, choosing appropriate scales so that the graph fills most of the grid.

(Additional graph paper, if required, will be found on *Page forty*.)

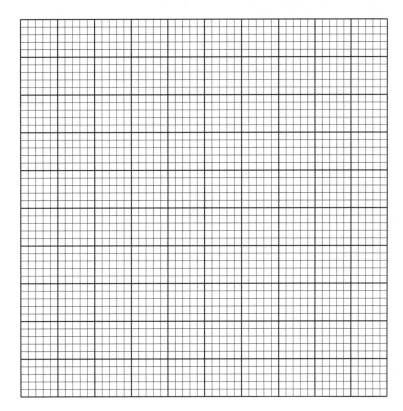

2

(e) The mass of the snail was 5·0 g.

Use results in the table to calculate the rate of oxygen uptake by the snail over the 10 minute period.

Space for calculation

_____ cm³ oxygen per minute per gram of snail　　1

(f) Explain how the respiration of the snail and the presence of the solution in the apparatus accounts for the movement of the coloured liquid on the scale.

_____

_____

_____

2

Marks

5. (*a*) Some clover plants are cyanogenic. These plants discourage grazing by releasing cyanide when their leaves are damaged by invertebrate herbivores. The map shows four zones of Europe with their average January temperatures. The pie-charts represent the percentages of cyanogenic and non-cyanogenic clover plants at sample sites in these zones.

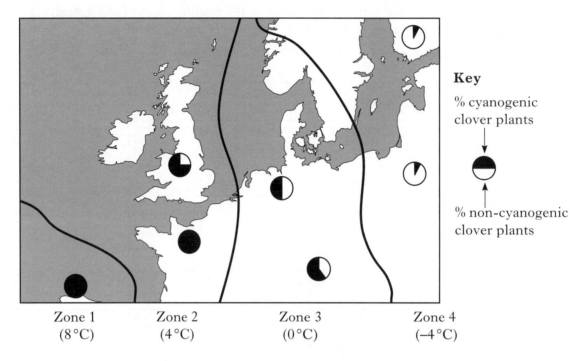

Zone 1 (8 °C)	Zone 2 (4 °C)	Zone 3 (0 °C)	Zone 4 (−4 °C)

Zones with their average January temperatures

(i) Describe the relationship between the percentages of cyanogenic clover plants and the average January temperature of the zone in which they occur.

_____

_____ 1

(ii) Zones with higher average January temperatures have higher densities of invertebrate herbivores.

Explain how this accounts for the distribution of the different clover varieties.

_____

_____

_____ 1

DO NOT
WRITE
IN THIS
MARGIN

Marks

5. (*a*) (continued)

(iii) Apart from cyanide, name **one** other toxic compound produced by plants to discourage grazing by herbivores.

_____   1

(iv) State **one** feature of some plant species which allows them to tolerate grazing by herbivores.

_____   1

(*b*) Name a substance produced by some plants which acts as a barrier to prevent the spread of infection from a wound site.

_____   1

[Turn over

Marks

6. (*a*) Peregrine falcons are predators which hunt wading birds such as redshank. In an investigation, the hunting success of peregrines and the sizes and distances of the feeding flocks of redshank from cover were recorded. The results are shown on the graph below.

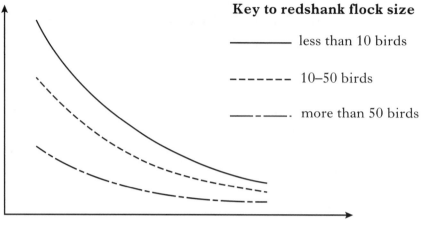

Key to redshank flock size

——————— less than 10 birds

- - - - - - 10–50 birds

—— - —— · more than 50 birds

Increasing distance of redshank from cover

Give **two** conclusions which can be drawn from the results.

1 _____

_____   1

2 _____

_____   1

(*b*) Hermit crabs withdraw into their shells if disturbed by small stones dropped into the water. If this harmless stimulus is repeated, the number of crabs responding decreases.

Name the type of behaviour shown by the crabs when they:

(i) withdraw into their shells;

_____   1

(ii) no longer respond to the repeated harmless stimulus.

_____   1

Marks

7. (a) The diagram shows a stage in meiosis in a cell from a Hawkweed plant.

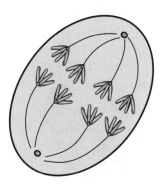

   (i) Name a structure in a Hawkweed flower in which meiosis occurs.

   _____   **1**

   (ii) In the following sentence, <u>underline</u> the word in the choice brackets which identifies the stage of meiosis shown and give a reason for your choice.

   This cell is from the $\begin{Bmatrix} \text{first} \\ \text{second} \end{Bmatrix}$ meiotic divison.

   Reason _____

   _____   **1**

   (iii) State the number of chromosomes which would be found in a gamete and in a gamete mother cell from this plant.

   gamete   _____

   gamete mother cell _____   **1**

   (b) Mutation during meiosis can lead to new phenotypes.

   (i) Other than mutation, state **one** feature of meiosis which can lead to the production of new phenotypes.

   _____   **1**

   (ii) Name the process which could result in the presence of an **extra** chromosome in a gamete.

   _____   **1**

[Turn over

Marks

8. Comb shape in chickens is determined by two genes located on **different** chromosomes. One of these genes has alleles **A** and **a** and the other has alleles **B** and **b**.

Single comb   Rose comb   Pea comb   Cushion comb

- Chickens without alleles **A** or **B** have single combs
- Chickens with allele **B** but not **A** have rose combs
- Chickens with allele **A** but not **B** have pea combs
- Chickens with alleles **A** and **B** have cushion combs

(a) A male heterozygous for both genes was crossed with a female with a single comb.   *e.g Bb*   ↑ AB

   (i) Complete the table below to show the parent genotypes and phenotypes and the genotypes of their gametes.

	Male	*Female*
Parent genotypes	AaBb	ab
Parent phenotypes	cushion comb	Single comb
Genotype(s) of gametes	A or a , B or b	ab

2

   (ii) Give the expected ratio of phenotypes for the offspring in this cross.

   Space for working

   _____ : _____ : _____ : _____

   cushion comb   rose comb   pea comb   single comb

1

(b) State the term used to describe genes which are found on the **same** chromosome.

   _____

1

Marks

9. In an investigation, 50 salmon were kept in a tank of fresh water for four days, then transferred to a tank of salt water for a further six days.

Each day, their gills were examined and the average diameter of chloride secretory cells was recorded.

The results are shown in the table below.

Contents of tank	Day	Average diameter of chloride secretory cells (micrometres)
Fresh water	1	203
	2	204
	3	202
	4	203
Salt water	5	280
	6	365
	7	471
	8	557
	9	615
	10	615

(a) In the following sentence, underline one alternative in each pair to make the sentence correct.

On day 3 the salmon are { hypertonic / hypotonic } to their surroundings and their chloride secretory cells actively transport salts { into / out of } the salmon.   1

(b) Describe the effect of salt water on the average diameter of the chloride secretory cells between day 5 and day 10.

_____

_____   2

(c) Following the investigation, the fish were returned to fresh water. In the table below, tick (✓) one box in each row to show how this change affects kidney function.

Kidney Function	Increases	Decreases	Stays the same
Filtration rate			
Urine concentration			
Urine volume			

2

10. French bean plants were grown over a period of four weeks in solutions containing different concentrations of lead ions.

After this period, measurements of transpiration rate, dry mass and lead content were taken from plants grown in each solution.

The **Graph** shows the average transpiration rate.

The **Table** shows the average dry masses of the roots and shoots.

The **Bar Chart** shows the average lead content of the roots and shoots.

Graph

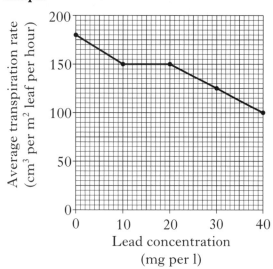

Table

Lead concentration (mg per l)	Average dry mass of roots (g)	Average dry mass of shoots (g)
0	3·1	0·4
10	3·2	0·3
20	2·2	0·2
30	2·0	0·1
40	1·3	0·1

Bar Chart

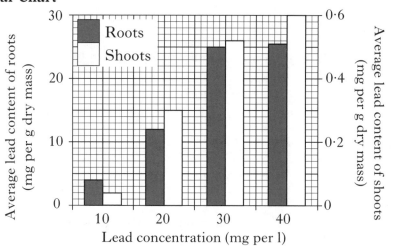

(a) (i) **Use values from the Graph** to describe the changes in average transpiration rate as the lead concentration increases from 0 to 40 mg per litre.

_____

_____

_____   2

(ii) What evidence from the **Graph** suggests that lead concentration is **not** the only factor affecting transpiration rate in this investigation?

_____

_____   1

Marks

DO NOT WRITE IN THIS MARGIN

DO NOT
WRITE
IN THIS
MARGIN

10. **(continued)**

Marks

(b) Use information from the **Table**, to calculate the percentage decrease in **combined** average dry mass of shoots **and** roots when the lead concentration in the solution was increased from 0 to 40 mg per litre.

Space for calculation

_____ % decrease   1

(c) Use information from the **Bar Chart** to:

(i) give the lead content of the shoots when the lead concentration of the solution was 10 mg per litre;

_____ mg per g dry mass   1

(ii) calculate the simplest whole number ratio of lead content in roots to shoots for plants grown in a solution of 20 mg lead per litre.

Space for calculation

_____ : _____
lead content in roots   lead content in shoots   1

(d) The lead content is expressed in mg of lead per gram of dry mass of the plant. Explain the advantage of using dry mass rather than fresh mass.

_____

_____

_____   1

(e) Using the **Table** and **Bar Chart**, calculate the average lead content of the roots of the plants grown in the solution containing 30 mg of lead per litre.

Space for calculation

_____ mg lead   1

(f) Explain why the presence of lead ions in the cells of French bean plants resulted in a decrease in growth.

_____

_____   2

Marks

11. (a) The graph shows the changes in body mass and height of a human male from the age of 1 to 21 years.

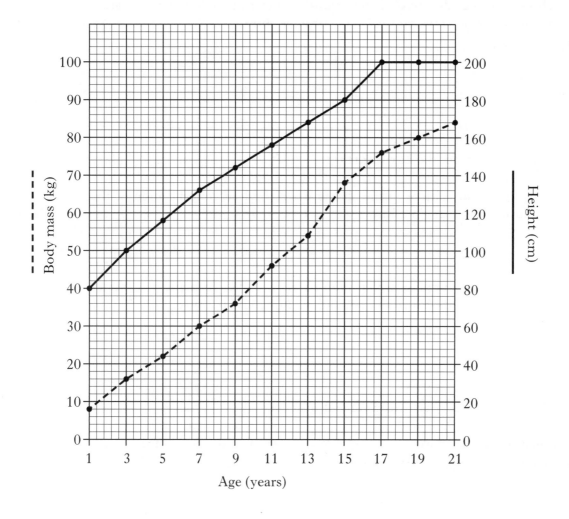

(i) Calculate the average yearly increase in body mass between 11 and 15 years.

Space for calculation

_____ kg   **1**

(ii) Tick (✓) the box to show the 4 year period in which the greatest increase in height occurred.

☐   ☐   ☐   ☐

1–5 years   5–9 years   9–13 years   13–17 years   **1**

11. (continued)

Marks

(b) The diagram shows how the pituitary gland is involved in the control of growth and development in humans.

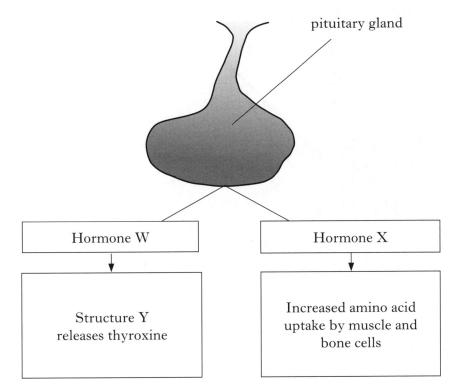

(i) Identify hormones W and X and structure Y.

Hormone W _____

Hormone X _____

Structure Y _____   2

(ii) Describe the effect of an increase in thyroxine production in humans.

_____

_____   1

[Turn over

12. (a) The diagram shows a vertical section through a shoot.

Marks

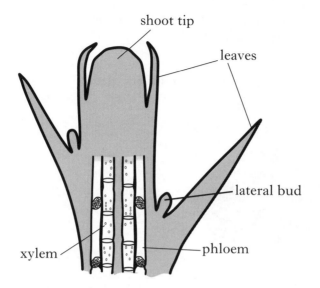

shoot tip

leaves

lateral bud

xylem

phloem

(i) Cells in the shoot tip produce indole acetic acid (IAA).

1   Describe how the IAA affects cellular activity resulting in an increase in shoot length.

_____

_____   1

2   Growth of lateral buds is inhibited by IAA.

State the term which describes this effect.

_____   1

(ii) Phloem and xylem are produced by the differentiation of unspecialised cells.

State how the differentiation of cells can be controlled by gene activity.

_____

_____

_____   1

(b) Macro-elements are important in the growth of plants.

(i) State the importance of magnesium in the growth of plants.

_____   1

(ii) Deficiency of phosphorus reduces overall growth of plants.

Give **one** other symptom of the deficiency of phosphorus in plants.

_____   1

Marks

13. The diagram shows an outline of the control of body temperature in a mammal.

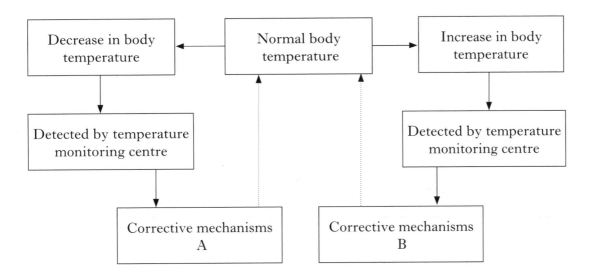

(*a*) (i) State the exact location of the temperature monitoring centre.

hypothalamus in brain

1

(ii) The skin has effectors which are involved in corrective mechanisms A and B.

State how messages are sent from the temperature monitoring centre to the skin.

nerve impulse

1

(iii) Give **one** example of a corrective mechanism B and explain how it would return the body temperature to normal.

*over
way
aroud*

Example *vasoconstriction*

1

Explanation *arterioles leading to skin
become constricted to reduce
heat & blood running to surfaces
reduos/*

1

(iv) Explain why maintaining body temperature within tolerable limits is important to the metabolism of mammals.

*so enzymes stay optimum temp &
do not denature*

1

(*b*) Mammals obtain most of their heat from their metabolism.

Give the term which describes animals that obtain most of their body heat from their surroundings.

conformer

1

Marks

14. (a) The diagram shows the relationship between a predator population and the population of its prey over a period of time.

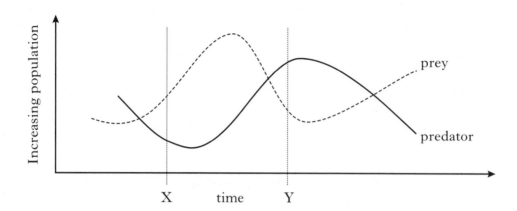

(i) Explain the changes in the population of **prey** between X and Y.

_____

_____

_____   2

(ii) Predation is a density-dependent factor.

Give **one** other density-dependent factor which influences animal populations.

_____   1

(b) Animal populations are monitored to provide data for a wide variety of purposes.

Complete the table to show the categories of species monitored and the use of the data collected.

Category of species	Use of data collected
	ensure future supply for human use
pest	
	assess levels of pollution
endangered	

2

Marks

15. (a) Flowering in some species of plant is affected by the periods of light and dark to which the plants are exposed.

The diagram below shows how flowering in plant species **P** and **Q** is affected by changing the periods of light and dark in 24 hours.

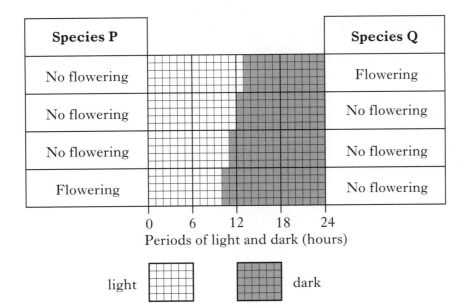

(i) <u>Underline</u> one alternative in each pair to make the sentence below correct.

Species **Q** is a $\left\{ \begin{array}{c} \text{long} \\ \text{short} \end{array} \right\}$ day plant which requires a critical dark

period of less than $\left\{ \begin{array}{c} \text{eleven} \\ \text{twelve} \end{array} \right\}$ hours to flower.   1

(ii) Predict the effect on the flowering of species **P** when exposed to the periods of light and dark shown below.

Justify your answer.

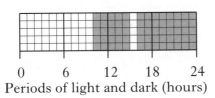

Prediction _____   1

Justification _____

_____   1

DO NOT
WRITE
IN THIS
MARGIN

15. (continued)

Marks

(b) (i) Ferrets are long day breeders and give birth six weeks after mating. Tick (✓) the box to show the season in which ferrets mate and explain how the timing of their breeding gives their offspring the best chance of survival.

Mating season   Spring ☐   Autumn ☐

Explanation _____

_____   1

(ii) What general term is used to describe the effect of light on the timing of breeding in mammals such as ferrets?

_____   1

Marks

SECTION C

Both questions in this section should be attempted.

Note that each question contains a choice.

Questions 1 and 2 should be attempted on the blank pages which follow.

Supplementary sheets, if required, may be obtained from the Invigilator.

All answers must be written clearly and legibly in ink.

Labelled diagrams may be used where appropriate.

1. Answer **either** A **or** B.

    A. Write notes on the evolution of new species under the following headings:

        (i) the role of isolation and mutation;   **6**

        (ii) natural selection.   **4**

        (10)

OR

    B. Write notes on adaptations for obtaining food in animals under the following headings:

        (i) the economics of foraging behaviour;   **2**

        (ii) cooperative hunting, dominance hierarchy and territorial behaviour.   **8**

        (10)

In question 2, ONE mark is available for coherence and ONE mark is available for relevance.

2. Answer **either** A **or** B.

    A. Give an account of the structure of a mitochondrion and the role of the cytochrome system in respiration.   **(10)**

    OR

    B. Give an account of phagocytosis and the role of lymphocytes in cellular defence.   **(10)**

[END OF QUESTION PAPER]

SPACE FOR ANSWERS

SPACE FOR ANSWERS

SPACE FOR ANSWERS

SPACE FOR ANSWERS

DO NOT
WRITE
IN THIS
MARGIN

SPACE FOR ANSWERS

SPACE FOR ANSWERS

SPACE FOR ANSWERS

ADDITIONAL GRAPH PAPER FOR QUESTION 4(*d*)

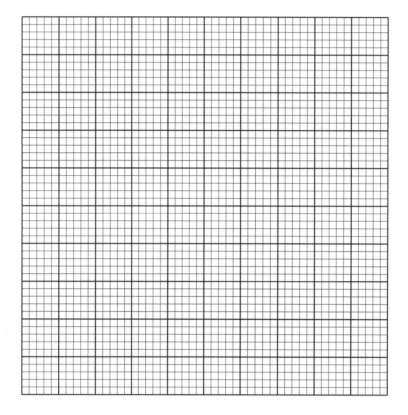

HIGHER

2013

[BLANK PAGE]

FOR OFFICIAL USE

Total for
Sections
B and C

X007/12/02

NATIONAL
QUALIFICATIONS
2013

WEDNESDAY, 15 MAY
1.00 PM – 3.30 PM

BIOLOGY
HIGHER

Fill in these boxes and read what is printed below.

Full name of centre

Town

Forename(s)

Surname

Date of birth

Day   Month   Year   Scottish candidate number   Number of seat

SECTION A—Questions 1—30 (30 Marks)

Instructions for completion of Section A are given on *Page two*.

For this section of the examination you must use an **HB pencil**.

SECTIONS B AND C (100 Marks)

1 (a) All questions should be attempted.

   (b) It should be noted that in **Section C** questions 1 and 2 each contain a choice.

2 The questions may be answered in any order but all answers are to be written in the spaces provided in this answer book, **and must be written clearly and legibly in ink**.

3 Additional space for answers will be found at the end of the book. If further space is required, supplementary sheets may be obtained from the Invigilator and should be inserted inside the **front** cover of this book.

4 The numbers of questions must be clearly inserted with any answers written in the additional space.

5 Rough work, if any should be necessary, should be written in this book and then scored through when the fair copy has been written. If further space is required, a supplementary sheet for rough work may be obtained from the Invigilator.

6 Before leaving the examination room you must give this book to the Invigilator. If you do not, you may lose all the marks for this paper.

Read carefully

1   Check that the answer sheet provided is for **Biology Higher (Section A)**.

2   For this section of the examination you must use an **HB pencil**, and where necessary, an eraser.

3   Check that the answer sheet you have been given has **your name**, **date of birth**, **SCN** (Scottish Candidate Number) and **Centre Name** printed on it.

    Do not change any of these details.

4   If any of this information is wrong, tell the Invigilator immediately.

5   If this information is correct, **print** your name and seat number in the boxes provided.

6   The answer to each question is **either** A, B, C or D. Decide what your answer is, then, using your pencil, put a horizontal line in the space provided (see sample question below).

7   There is **only one correct** answer to each question.

8   Any rough working should be done on the question paper or the rough working sheet, **not** on your answer sheet.

9   At the end of the examination, put the **answer sheet for Section A inside the front cover of this answer book**.

Sample Question

The apparatus used to determine the energy stored in a foodstuff is a

A   calorimeter

B   respirometer

C   klinostat

D   gas burette.

The correct answer is **A**—calorimeter. The answer **A** has been clearly marked in **pencil** with a horizontal line (see below).

Changing an answer

If you decide to change your answer, carefully erase your first answer and using your pencil fill in the answer you want. The answer below has been changed to **D**.

SECTION A

All questions in this section should be attempted.

Answers should be given on the separate answer sheet provided.

1. Plant cell walls are composed mainly of

   A   cellulose

   B   phospholipid

   C   collagen

   D   starch.

2. Visking tubing is selectively permeable. In the experiment shown below to demonstrate osmosis, the following results were obtained.

   Initial mass of Visking tubing
   + contents   = 10·0 g

   Mass of Visking tubing + contents
   after experiment   = 11·8 g

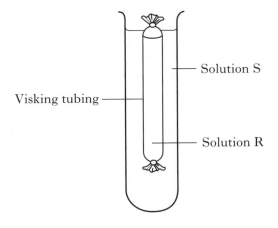

   The results shown could be obtained when

   A   R is a 5% salt solution and S is a 10% salt solution

   B   R is a 10% salt solution and S is a 5% salt solution

   C   R is water and S is a 10% salt solution

   D   R is water and S is a 5% salt solution.

3. The diagram below represents part of the Calvin cycle within a chloroplast.

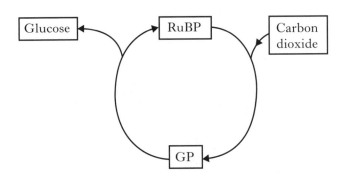

   Which line in the table below shows the effect of decreasing CO_2 availability on the concentrations of RuBP and GP in the cycle?

	RuBP concentration	GP concentration
A	decrease	decrease
B	increase	increase
C	decrease	increase
D	increase	decrease

[Turn over

4. Which of the following must be present in a living cell for glycolysis to occur?

   A   Glucose and ATP

   B   Pyruvic acid and oxygen

   C   Glucose and oxygen

   D   Pyruvic acid and ATP

5. Which of the following chemical changes in cells results in the synthesis of most ATP?

   A   Glucose to pyruvic acid

   B   Pyruvic acid to lactic acid

   C   Pyruvic acid to acetyl group

   D   Pyruvic acid to carbon dioxide and water

6. The graph below shows the effect of the carbon dioxide concentration of inhaled air on the breathing rate of an individual.

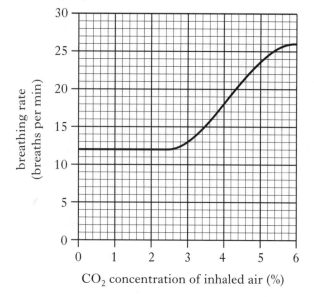

CO$_2$ concentration of inhaled air (%)

If the volume of one breath is 0·5 litre, what volume of air will be breathed in one minute when the CO$_2$ concentration is 4%?

   A   6 litres

   B   9 litres

   C   18 litres

   D   36 litres

7. If ten percent of the bases in a molecule of DNA are adenine, what is the ratio of adenine to guanine in the same molecule?

   A   1:1

   B   1:2

   C   1:3

   D   1:4

8. The diagram below shows some structures within an animal cell.

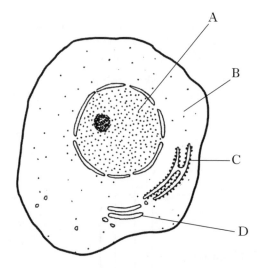

Where does synthesis of messenger RNA take place?

9. The processing of proteins prior to secretion takes place in the

   A   endoplasmic reticulum

   B   Golgi apparatus

   C   ribosomes

   D   vesicles.

10. Phagocytes contain lysosomes that

   A   recognise foreign antigens on bacteria

   B   produce antibodies to destroy viruses

   C   surround and engulf invading viruses

   D   contain enzymes which destroy bacteria.

11. In garden pea plants the genes for height and flower colour are on different chromosomes. The allele **T** (tall) is dominant to the allele **t** (dwarf) and the allele **R** (purple flowers) is dominant to the allele **r** (white flowers).

A true-breeding tall plant with purple flowers was crossed with a dwarf plant with white flowers.

The F_1 generation were self-pollinated and 64 plants were obtained in the F_2 generation.

How many of the F_2 generation would be expected to be tall with white flowers?

A   36

B   16

C   12

D   4

12. Which line in the table correctly shows characteristics of mutant alleles?

	Frequency	Occurrence
A	high	random
B	high	non-random
C	low	random
D	low	non-random

13. Which of the following has occurred as a result of natural selection?

A   Modern varieties of potato have been produced from wild varieties.

B   Ayrshire cows have been bred to increase milk yield.

C   Bacteria have developed resistance to some antibiotics.

D   Some tomato plants produced by somatic fusion have resistance to fungal diseases.

14. The dark variety of the peppered moth became common in industrial areas of Britain following the increase in production of soot during the Industrial Revolution.

The increase in the dark form was due to

A   dark moths migrating to areas which offered the best camouflage

B   a change in the prey species taken by birds

C   an increase in the mutation rate

D   a change in selection pressure.

15. An eel was transferred from salt water to fresh water.

The table shows how the drinking rate of the eel changed in the six hour period after transfer.

Time after transfer (hours)	Drinking rate (cm^3 per kg body mass per hour)
0	20
1	17
2	15
3	12
4	10
5	8
6	2

What is the average hourly decrease in drinking rate over the six hour period after transfer?

A   3 cm^3 per kg body mass per hour

B   12 cm^3 per kg body mass per hour

C   14 cm^3 per kg body mass per hour

D   18 cm^3 per kg body mass per hour

[Turn over

16. Which line in the table below describes the action of chloride secretory cells in the gills and the glomerular filtration rate of a salmon living in sea water?

	Action of chloride secretory cells in the gills	Glomerular filtration rate
A	excretes salts	high
B	excretes salts	low
C	absorbs salts	low
D	absorbs salts	high

17. The diagram below shows a stoma and its guard cells in the lower epidermis of a leaf.

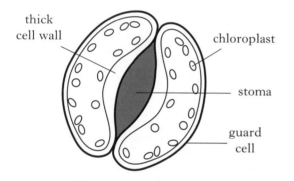

thick cell wall

chloroplast

stoma

guard cell

Which line of the table below describes the conditions which result in the stoma being fully open as shown in the diagram?

	Lighting conditions	Condition of guard cells
A	light	flaccid
B	dark	flaccid
C	light	turgid
D	dark	turgid

18. The Soft Brome grass and the Storksbill are species of plant which grow in the grasslands of California. The Storksbill has a more extensive root system, but does not grow as tall as the Soft Brome grass.

From this information, in which of the following conditions would the Storksbill be expected to survive better than Soft Brome grass?

A   Drought

B   High soil moisture levels

C   High light intensity

D   Shade

19. Two plants of different species had their carbon dioxide (CO_2) uptake and output measured in relation to light intensity. The results are shown below.

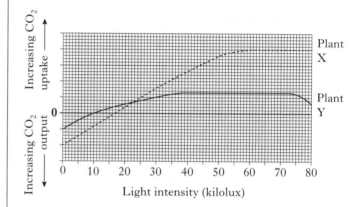

Which line in the table below is a correct interpretation of the graph?

	Type of plant	Light intensity at which compensation point is reached
A	X is a shade plant	17 kilolux
B	X is a sun plant	60 kilolux
C	Y is a shade plant	10 kilolux
D	Y is a sun plant	40 kilolux

20. A substitution mutation in a gene results in a triplet of bases TTC being changed to TCC. The amino acid lysine is coded for by TTC and arginine is coded for by TCC.

    The effect of this mutation on the resulting protein would be that

    A all lysine molecules would be replaced by arginine molecules throughout the protein

    B one lysine molecule would replace arginine at one point in the protein

    C all arginine molecules would be replaced by lysine molecules throughout the protein

    D one arginine molecule would replace lysine at one point in the protein.

21. The diagram below shows a section through a young plant stem. In which region would a meristem be found?

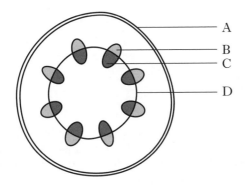

22. The ability of a plant to replace damaged parts through new growth is called

    A abscission

    B regeneration

    C differentiation

    D apical dominance.

23. Which of the following statements best defines the term population density?

    A The number of individuals of a species present per unit area of a habitat.

    B The number of individuals of all species present in a habitat.

    C The maximum number of individuals of all species which the resources of a habitat can support.

    D The maximum number of individuals of a species which the resources of a habitat can support.

24. The apparatus shown below was used to investigate the effects of phosphate on the growth of grass seedlings.

    The experiment was repeated using different concentrations of phosphate and the height of the seedlings was recorded after 6 weeks of growth.

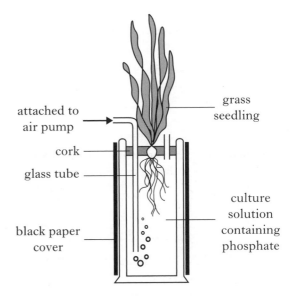

    Two variables that must be kept the same are

    A temperature and concentration of phosphate in the culture solution

    B concentration of phosphate in the culture solution and light intensity

    C light intensity and temperature

    D temperature and the height of the seedlings.

25. Liver tissue contains an enzyme which breaks down alcohol. The graph below shows the effect of different concentrations of copper ions on the breakdown of alcohol by this enzyme over a 30 minute period.

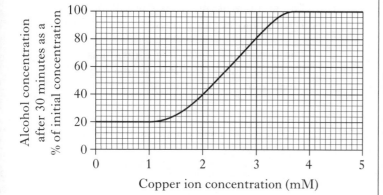

Which of the following conclusions can be drawn from the graph?

A   4·5 mM copper has no effect on enzyme activity.

B   2·5 mM copper halves the enzyme activity.

C   0·5 mM copper completely inhibits enzyme activity.

D   Enzyme activity increases when copper concentration is increased from 1 mM to 2 mM.

26. Which line in the table below correctly identifies the substances required for normal blood-clotting and for the prevention of rickets?

	Normal blood-clotting	Prevention of rickets
A	calcium	vitamin D
B	vitamin D	calcium
C	iron	vitamin D
D	calcium	iron

27. Nicotine is a chemical which may affect fetal development.

The diagram shows the stages of development when major and minor malformations of organs may occur if there is exposure to nicotine during the first twelve weeks of pregnancy.

Key   ▮ major malformation
      ▨ minor malformation

Organ	Stage of development (weeks of pregnancy)											
	1	2	3	4	5	6	7	8	9	10	11	12
brain			▮	▮	▮	▨	▨	▨	▨	▨		
ear				▮	▮	▮	▮	▮	▨	▨	▨	▨
limbs				▮	▮	▮	▨					
genitalia							▮	▮	▮	▨	▨	▨

For how many weeks during pregnancy is there a possibility of major malformations to organs during development?

A   6

B   7

C   9

D   14

28. A species of short-day plant only flowers if the number of hours of continuous darkness in its 24 hour cycle is at least at the critical value shown in chart below.

24 hour cycle

Light   Dark

Critical value

Three plants of this species were exposed to different photoperiods as shown below.

Plant 1   Plant 2   Plant 3

Which plant(s) would be expected to flower?

A   1 only

B   2 only

C   1 and 2 only

D   2 and 3 only

29. The diagram below shows a section through the skin of a mammal.

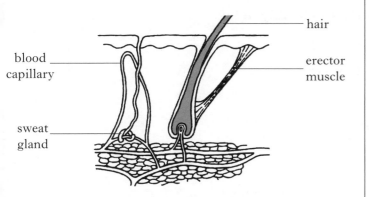

Which line in the table below correctly identifies the state of the erector muscle and the change in blood flow in the capillary which would be expected if the skin was exposed to low temperature?

	State of erector muscle	Change to blood flow in capillary
A	contracted	increase
B	contracted	decrease
C	relaxed	increase
D	relaxed	decrease

30. Which of the following factors influencing population change in an animal species is density-independent?

A   Disease

B   Food availability

C   Temperature

D   Predation

Candidates are reminded that the answer sheet MUST be returned INSIDE the front cover of this answer book.

[Turn over for SECTION B on *Page ten*

SECTION B

Marks

All questions in this section should be attempted.

All answers must be written clearly and legibly in ink.

1. (*a*) The diagram below shows part of a DNA molecule.

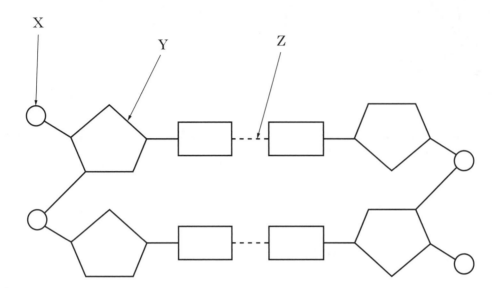

    (i) Name components X and Y.

       X   *Phosphate group*

       Y   *Deoxyribose sugar.*   1

    (ii) Name the type of bond shown at Z.

        Hydrogen   1

DO NOT
WRITE
IN THIS
MARGIN

Marks

1. **(continued)**

    (*b*) (i) The flowchart below describes steps in the process of DNA replication.

    Complete the boxes to describe what happens at **Step 2** and **Step 4**.

Step 1	Original DNA double helix unwinds.

⇩

Step 2	

⇩

Step 3	Free DNA nucleotides bond with complementary nucleotides on the original DNA strands.

⇩

Step 4	

⇩

Step 5	Double strands twist and two new DNA double helices are formed.

2

    (ii) Other than the original DNA strand and free DNA nucleotides, give **one** substance needed for DNA replication.

    _____   1

    (iii) State the importance of DNA replication to cells.

    _____

    _____

    _____   1

Marks

2. (*a*) Cherry tree leaves are attacked by greenfly. The leaves contain cyanogenic glycosides which are broken down to release cyanide when greenfly damage them. The cyanide acts as a defence against **most** greenfly species.

The graph below shows the average number of individuals of a species of greenfly per leaf and the concentration of cyanogenic glycosides in the leaves of a cherry tree over a 60 day period.

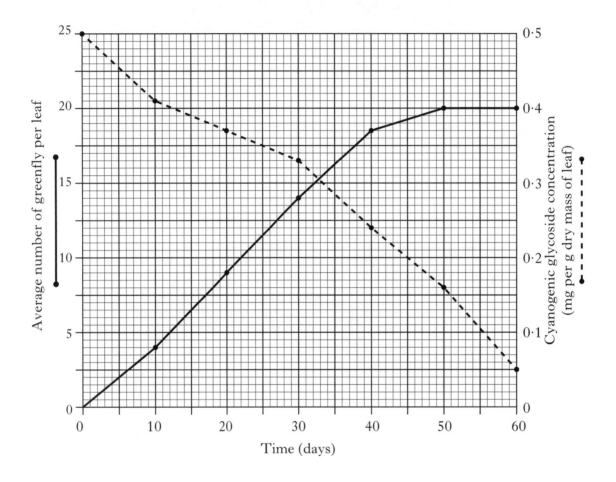

(i) Explain how changes in the population of greenfly account for the fall in the cyanogenic glycoside concentration throughout the period.

_____

_____

_____   2

(ii) What evidence is there that this greenfly species is resistant to the effects of cyanide?

_____   1

DO NOT WRITE IN THIS MARGIN

Marks

2. (*a*) (continued)

(iii) Calculate the average increase **per day** in the number of greenfly per leaf between day 10 and day 50.

Space for calculation

Average increase per day ______________________ **1**

(iv) State the cyanogenic glycoside concentration when the average number of greenfly per leaf was 14.

______________________ mg per gram dry mass of leaf **1**

(*b*) Some plants secrete sticky resin in response to damage.

Explain how resin protects the plants.

____

____ **1**

[Turn over

DO NOT
WRITE
IN THIS
MARGIN

Marks

3. The diagram shows a cell from the root epidermis of the Spanish reed.

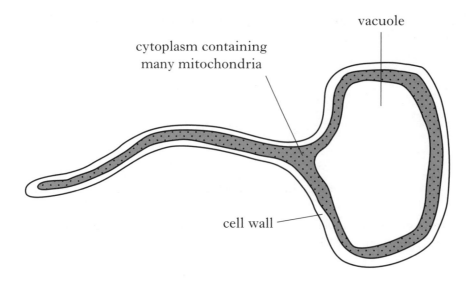

vacuole

cytoplasm containing
many mitochondria

cell wall

(a) Name this type of cell and describe how it is adapted for the absorption of
    water from the soil.

    Type of cell _____   **1**

    Description _____

    _____   **1**

(b) The Spanish reed is adapted to grow in soil with high salt concentration. Salt
    enters the plant due to its high concentration in the soil. In order to survive,
    the plant must remove the excess salt from its cells.

    Name the process by which the salt is removed and describe the role of
    mitochondria in this process.

    Process _____   **1**

    Role of mitochondria in this process _____

    _____

    _____   **1**

[Turn over for Question 4 on *Page sixteen*

4. In an investigation into the effect of lead ion concentration on respiration in yeast, *Marks* two flasks were set up as described below.

Flask	Contents
A	200 cm^3 glucose solution + 5 cm^3 0·2% lead nitrate solution
B	200 cm^3 glucose solution + 5 cm^3 1·0% lead nitrate solution

The flasks were placed in a water bath at 20 °C for 10 minutes. After this time 2·5 cm^3 of yeast suspension was added to each and oxygen sensors fitted as shown in the diagram below.

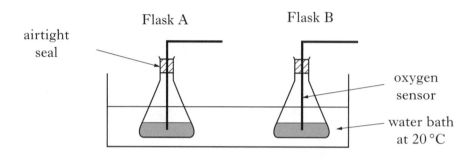

The flasks were left for a **further** 10 minutes and then oxygen concentration was measured in each flask every 20 seconds for 2 minutes.

The results are shown in the table below.

Time (s)	Oxygen concentration (mg per litre)	
	Flask A 0·2% lead nitrate	Flask B 1·0% lead nitrate
0	10·2	10·8
20	8·4	9·3
40	6·1	7·6
60	3·8	6·2
80	1·7	5·1
100	0·2	4·0
120	0·0	3·2

(a) (i) Identify **one** variable, not already mentioned, which would have to be kept constant so that valid conclusions could be drawn.

_____   1

    (ii) Explain why the flasks were left for 10 minutes **before** the yeast suspension was added.

_____

_____   1

4. (a) (continued)

Marks

   (iii) Explain why the flasks were left for a **further** 10 minutes after the yeast suspensions were added before measurement of oxygen concentrations were taken.

_____

_____ 1

(b) On the grid provided, draw a line graph to show the oxygen concentration in **Flask A** against time. Use an appropriate scale to fill most of the grid. (Additional graph paper, if required, will be found on Page forty.)

2

(c) Using information from the table, state the effect of increasing lead ion concentration on the aerobic respiration of yeast.

_____

_____ 1

(d) Bubbles of gas appeared in both flasks throughout the investigation.

   (i) Name this gas.

_____ 1

   (ii) Explain why this gas continued to be produced in **Flask A** at 120s.

_____

_____ 1

Marks

5. (a) The diagram below shows two pairs of homologous chromosomes from a cell
dividing by meiosis in a flowering plant. The letters represent alleles.

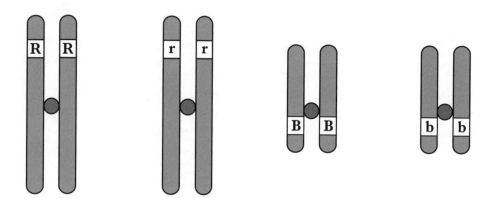

(i) Use letters from the diagram to give the genotypes of all four possible
gametes which could be produced by this plant.

_____   _____   _____   _____   1

(ii) The diagram below shows the same pairs of homologous chromosomes
separating during the first meiotic division.

The position of **one** of the alleles is shown.

Complete the diagram by adding letters to the remaining boxes to show
the positions of the alleles that would result in the production of a
gamete with the genotype **Rb**.

spindle
fibre

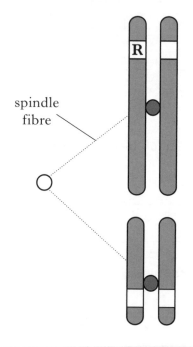   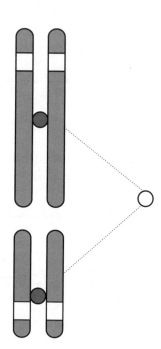

1

DO NOT
WRITE
IN THIS
MARGIN

Marks

5. (*a*) (continued)

(iii) The chromosomes shown have two copies of each gene.

Describe what occurs during the second meiotic division which results in every gamete produced having only one copy of each gene.

_____

_____   **1**

(*b*) The diagram below shows another pair of homologous chromosomes from the same plant cell.

The letters for the alleles of two linked genes are shown.

 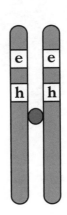

(i) The grid below shows the genotypes of the possible gametes produced by this cell following meiosis.

Complete the grid by ticking (✓) the boxes to show which of the gametes produced are recombinants.

Genotype of gametes	EH	Eh	eH	eh
Recombinant gametes				

1

(ii) Name the process that occurs during meiosis that results in the production of recombinant gametes.

State the importance of this process to the plant species.

Process _____   **1**

Importance _____

_____   **1**

Marks

6. (*a*) The map below shows the locations of six populations of the house mouse on the island of Madeira.

Studies on the mice have shown that speciation is occurring.

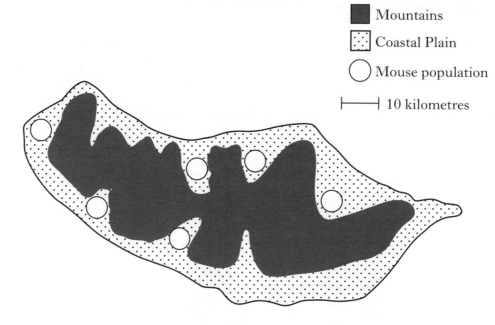

■ Mountains

▨ Coastal Plain

◯ Mouse population

├──┤ 10 kilometres

(i) Using information in the diagram, name the isolating mechanism involved in speciation of the mice.

_____   **1**

(ii) Explain the importance of isolating mechanisms in the evolution of a new species.

_____

_____   **1**

(iii) Describe evidence which would confirm that the populations of mice had evolved to become separate species.

_____

_____   **1**

Marks

6. **(continued)**

(b) **Diagram A** shows a bacterial plasmid containing genes for resistance to the antibiotics tetracycline and ampicillin.

Diagram B shows this plasmid after it had been genetically engineered by inserting a human blood-clotting gene.

Diagram A

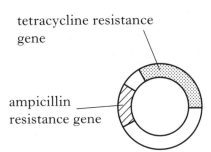

tetracycline resistance gene

ampicillin resistance gene

Diagram B

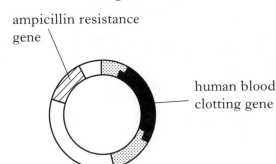

ampicillin resistance gene

human blood clotting gene

(i) Give a technique which could be used to locate the position of the blood-clotting gene on a human chromosome.

_____ 1

(ii) Two different enzymes are used to produce the genetically engineered plasmid.

Complete the table to show the function of each enzyme.

Enzyme	*Function*
endonuclease	
ligase	

2

(iii) The genetically engineered plasmids were inserted into bacteria.

Using information from the diagrams, explain why these bacteria were **not** resistant to tetracycline.

_____

_____

_____ 2

Marks

7. Red-green colour deficiency in humans is caused by a mutation in the gene coding for one of the proteins needed for normal colour vision.

This gene is sex-linked and the allele for colour deficiency **d** is recessive to the allele for normal colour vision **D**.

The diagram below shows inheritance of red-green colour deficiency in a family.

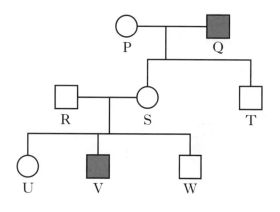

■ Affected male

□ Unaffected male

◯ Unaffected female

(*a*) Give the genotype of each of the following individuals.

Q _____

S _____

W _____

2

(*b*) Explain how information from the diagram confirms that the allele causing red-green colour deficiency is recessive.

_____

_____

_____

1

(*c*) Explain why males are more likely to be affected by red-green colour deficiency than females.

_____

_____

_____

1

Marks

8. (*a*) Marram grass is adapted to reduce water loss. Its leaves contain hinge cells which let them curl when the soil in which the plant grows is dry.

When the soil is moist, the hinge cells make the leaves uncurl.

The diagram below shows a section through a **curled** leaf of marram grass.

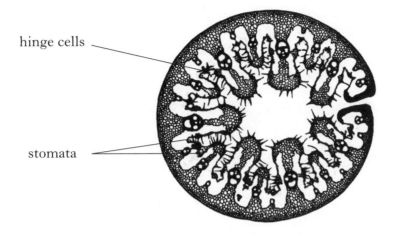

hinge cells

stomata

(i) Explain how curling of the leaves helps to reduce water loss from marram grass.

_____

_____

_____   **2**

(ii) The rate of photosynthesis in marram grass leaves increases when the soil is moist.

Explain how the action of the hinge cells contributes to this increase.

_____

_____

_____   **2**

(iii) Give the term used to describe a plant which has adaptations to reduce water loss.

_____   **1**

DO NOT
WRITE
IN THIS
MARGIN

Marks

8. (continued)

(*b*) The table below shows features found in plants adapted to grow in water.

Explain the advantages of each feature to the plants by completing the table.

Feature	Advantage to plant
Large air spaces between leaf cells	
Flexible stems	

2

Marks

9. The diagram below shows a section through a barley grain and the location of events occurring during germination.

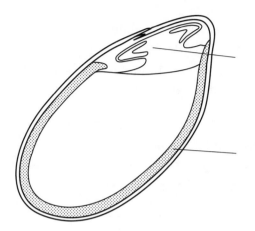

Growth substance P produced

Growth substance P induces aleurone layer to produce α-amylase

(a) Name growth substance P and the site of its production.

Name _____

Site of production _____   **1**

(b) Give the function of α-amylase and explain the importance of its action in the germination and early growth of barley grains.

Function _____   **1**

Importance _____

_____

_____   **1**

[Turn over

10. Rufous hummingbirds migrate thousands of kilometres each year between their summer breeding areas in Canada and their wintering areas in Mexico.

Marks

They feed on nectar throughout the year and are strongly territorial even on migration.

The birds save energy at night by entering a temporary state known as torpor in which body temperature and respiration rate are greatly reduced.

The **chart** below shows the average body mass of the hummingbirds and the average number of hours per night spent in torpor throughout the year.

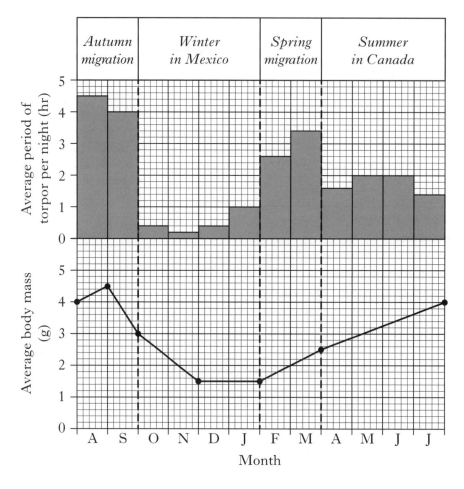

(*a*) (i) **Use values from the chart** to describe the changes in average body mass of the hummingbirds from the beginning of August until the end of January.

_____

_____

_____

_____   2

(ii) Calculate the percentage increase in average body mass during the summer in Canada.

Space for calculation

_____ %   **1**

10. **(a)** **(continued)**

    (iii) Suggest **one** reason for the changes in average body mass of the birds during the summer in Canada.

_____

_____ **1**

(b)   (i) Explain why the increased time spent in torpor during migration is an advantage to the birds.

_____

_____ **1**

    (ii) Suggest a reason why the periods of torpor are longer in the summer than the winter.

_____

_____ **1**

   (iii) Calculate the average period of torpor per month throughout the winter in Mexico.

Space for calculation

_____ hours per night   **1**

(c) The **table** below shows how the average oxygen consumption of the birds at rest is affected by their body temperature.

Body temperature	*Average oxygen consumption at rest* (cm^3 per gram of body mass per hour)
Normal	15·0
Lowered during torpor	2·0

Using information from the **chart** and the **table**, calculate the average volume of oxygen consumed per hour by a hummingbird at the end of September at normal body temperature.

Space for calculation

_____ cm^3 **1**

(d) Give the advantage to rufous hummingbirds of territorial behaviour.

_____

_____ **1**

Marks

11. At the start of an investigation, the blood glucose and insulin concentrations of a healthy adult human were measured and found to be normal. The individual then immediately drank a glucose drink and his blood glucose and insulin levels were re-measured at intervals over a period of 5 hours without further food or drink intake.

The results are shown in the table below.

Time after glucose drink was taken (hours)	Glucose concentration (mg per 100 cm^3)	Insulin concentration (units)
0 (start)	80	50
0·5	90	550
1	120	500
2	100	400
3	80	100
4	80	50
5	70	45

(a) Calculate the simplest whole number ratio of blood glucose concentration at the start to the maximum level recorded.

Space for calculation

_____ at start : _____ at maximum level   1

(b) Calculate how long it took for blood insulin concentration to return to the start level from its maximum concentration.

Space for calculation

_____ hours   1

(c) Give **two** reasons to account for the decrease in blood glucose concentration between 1 and 3 hours.

1 _____

_____

2 _____

_____   2

(d) Predict how the individual's blood glucagon concentration will change after 5 hours assuming no further intake of food or drink. Explain the importance of this.

Prediction _____

Explanation _____

_____   2

Marks

12. (*a*) The graph below shows the changes in body mass and mass of growth hormone (GH) in the blood of a human from birth to age 24 years.

Age (years)

(i) Tick (✓) the box to show the age range during which the most rapid increase in body mass occurred.

0–2 years   2–12 years   12–18 years   18–24 years

☐   ☐   ☐   ☐   **1**

(ii) An increase in growth hormone (GH) causes an increase in mass of muscle and bone tissues.

Tick (✓) the box to show the region of the graph which **best** supports this statement.

W   X   Y   Z

☐   ☐   ☐   ☐   **1**

(iii) Factors other than growth hormone (GH) are involved in increases in body mass in humans.

Describe how the graph supports this statement.

_____

_____   **1**

(*b*) Name the site of the production of growth hormone (GH) in humans.

_____   **1**

Marks

13. In an experiment to investigate the Jacob-Monod hypothesis of lactose metabolism in *E. coli*, flasks were set up as shown in the diagram below.

Flask 1   Flask 2

— Cotton wool plug

E. coli + nutrient solution   *E. coli* + nutrient solution
with lactose   without lactose

E. coli breaks down lactose using the enzyme β–galactosidase as shown.

$$\text{Lactose} \xrightarrow{\beta\text{–galactosidase}} \text{glucose} + \text{galactose}$$

(a) (i) β–galactosidase was produced in **Flask 1**.

Describe events which led to the production of this enzyme.

_____

_____

_____

_____   2

(ii) β–galactosidase was **not** produced in **Flask 2**.

Explain the advantage to *E. coli* of **not** producing the enzyme in this case.

_____

_____   1

(b) ONPG is a colourless substance which is converted to a yellow product by β–galactosidase.

Use this information to describe how ONPG could be used to show that *E. coli* only produced β–galactosidase in the presence of lactose.

_____

_____   1

Marks

14. In an investigation, young plant shoots were exposed to 48 hours of light from above or from one side only.

Their growth responses are shown in the diagrams below.

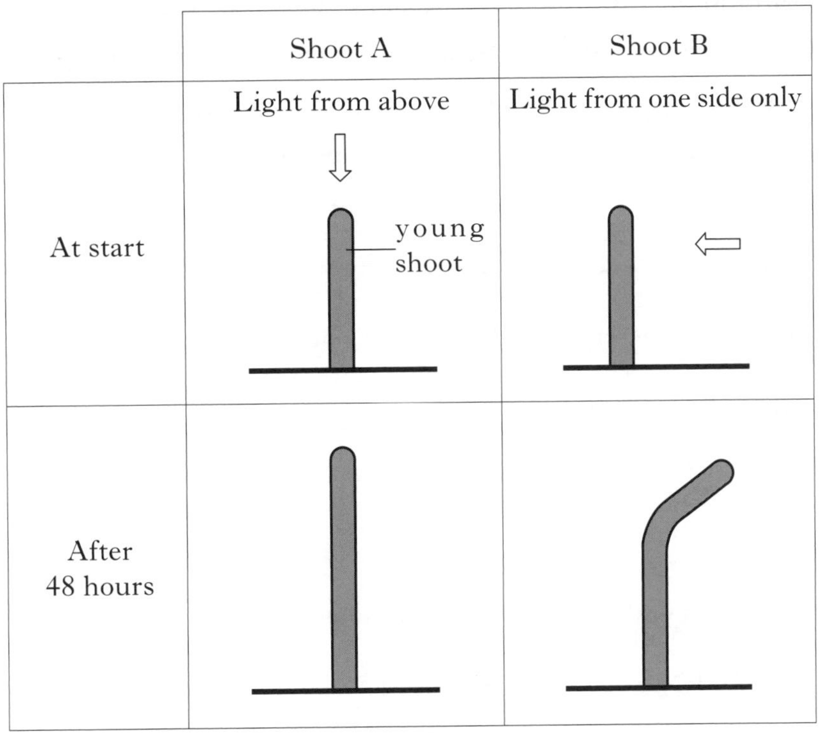

(a) Name the response shown by the shoots and explain the advantage of this response to the plants.

Name _____   **1**

Advantage _____

_____   **1**

(b) (i) Light from one side causes elongating cells to receive an uneven distribution of a growth substance produced by the shoot tip.

Use this information to explain the growth response of **shoot B** after 48 hours.

_____

_____

_____   **2**

(ii) Name the growth substance produced by the shoot tip which is involved in this growth response to light.

_____   **1**

[Turn over for SECTION C on *Page thirty-two*

Marks

SECTION C

Both questions in this section should be attempted.

Note that each question contains a choice.

Questions 1 and 2 should be attempted on the blank pages which follow.

Supplementary sheets, if required, may be obtained from the Invigilator.

All answers must be written clearly and legibly in ink.

Labelled diagrams may be used where appropriate.

1. Answer **either** A **or** B.

    A. Write notes on photosynthesis under the following headings:

    (i)   role of light and photosynthetic pigments;   **4**

    (ii) light dependent stage.   **6**

                                                                                   (10)

    OR

    B. Write notes on proteins under the following headings:

    (i)   translation of mRNA in protein synthesis;   **7**

    (ii) the types and functions of protein.   **3**

                                                                                   (10)

In question 2, ONE mark is available for coherence and ONE mark is available for relevance.

2. Answer **either** A **or** B.

    A. Give an account of the regulation of blood water content in mammals following a decrease in blood water concentration.   **(10)**

    OR

    B. Give an account of the process of succession in plant communities and the reasons for monitoring wild populations.   **(10)**

[END OF QUESTION PAPER]

SPACE FOR ANSWERS

SPACE FOR ANSWERS

DO NOT
WRITE
IN THIS
MARGIN

SPACE FOR ANSWERS

SPACE FOR ANSWERS

Page thirty-six

DO NOT
WRITE
IN THIS
MARGIN

SPACE FOR ANSWERS

SPACE FOR ANSWERS

SPACE FOR ANSWERS

SPACE FOR ANSWERS

ADDITIONAL GRAPH PAPER FOR QUESTION 4 (*b*)

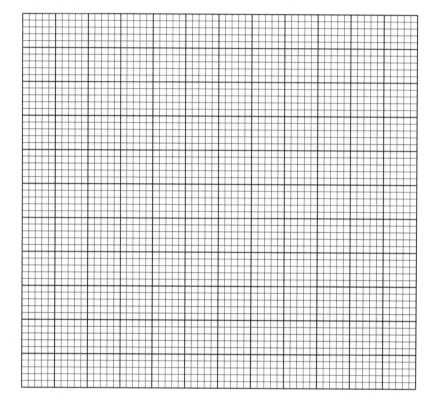

HIGHER | ANSWER SECTION

SQA HIGHER BIOLOGY
2009–2013

Section A

1.	B	16.	B
2.	A	17.	C
3.	D	18.	D
4.	B	19.	A
5.	B	20.	D
6.	C	21.	D
7.	C	22.	B
8.	D	23.	D
9.	B	24.	A
10.	B	25.	C
11.	C	26.	A
12.	A	27.	A
13.	D	28.	C
14.	A	29.	C
15.	C	30.	D

Section B

1. (a) Y transmitted/transmission/transmit

   Z reflected/reflection/reflect (both)

   (b) (i) Chlorophyll/chlorophyll a/chlorophyll b

   (ii) Widen/broaden absorption spectrum
   OR
   Absorb different colours/named colours
   Use other wavelengths
   AND pass energy on to chlorophyll

   (c) (i) Stroma (of chloroplast)

   (ii) To reduce/reduction of GP/CO_2

   (d) P temperature
   Q carbon dioxide/CO_2 (concentration)
   R temperature
   OR light intensity

2. (a) (i) W oxygen/O_2
   X acetyl (group)
   Y carbon dioxide/CO_2

   (ii) 6

   (b) (i) 10 hours

   (ii) 3·5

3. (a) (i) Translation

   (ii) Peptide

   (iii) 1 proline
   4 glycine

   (b) (Many) Golgi apparatus/vesicles/bodies

4. (a) (i) Protein (coat)

   (ii) Virus takes over cell/host metabolism

(iii) *Any two from:*
   1. viral nucleic acid/DNA/RNA transcribed to/directs synthesis of mRNA
   2. mRNA translated into protein coats
   3. viruses assembled/put together

   (b) (i) (Foreign) Antigen

   (ii) 1. 3·75 times

   2. 1. (Response) is quicker/faster/took less time
   2. (Antibody concentration) remains high for longer/decreased slower/maintained at higher level for longer

5. (a) (i) 88%

   (ii) 88:19:4

   (b) Pair A
   Different numbers/less of woodrats **AND** brush mice in diet

   (c) (i) Increases/changes from 3·6 to 4·0 in summer (of year 1) then decreases/changes from 4·0 to 2·0 in winter (of year 2)
   Then increases/changes from 2·0 to 3·2 (in spring of year 2)

   (ii) 52%

   (d) 20g

   (e) In winter number **AND** biomass of prey is less so have bigger territory

6. (a) Ovaries/testes

   (b) (i) Chiasma/ata

   (ii) R and T
   T and R

   (iii) Independent assortment/segregation/alignment
   OR Random segregation/assortment/alignment

   (c) 40

7. (a) (i) BE, Be, bE, be

   (ii) 1 black: 1 chocolate: 2 yellow

   (b) bbEE/EEbb

8. (a) (i) As the cuticle thickness increases up to 5·6 (micrometers) the rate of water loss decreases = 1
   But further increase in cuticle thickness causes very little/no difference in rate of water loss = 1

   (ii) Turgid

   (iii) Increased temperature/warmer
   OR increased wind speed/windiness/windy conditions
   OR windier

   (b) (i) Reduces air movements
   OR traps water vapour/moist air/increased humidity = 1
   fewer stomata
   OR smaller surface area for evaporation/transpiration = 1

   (ii) Xerophytes/xerophytic

9. (a) (i) Biomass reduced because grass has been eaten/grazed/removed
   Increased diversity because reduced competition allows less vigorous/less dominant to survive/colonise/move in
   AND
   allows others/less vigorous/less dominant to survive/colonise/move in

(ii) Reduce/decrease the diversity
Some species would be completely eaten/unable to recover from grazing

(b) Ticks at dandelions and couch grass only

Plant adaptation	Tick (✓)
Dandelions have deep roots	✓
Wild roses have thorns	
Couch grass has underground stems	✓
Nettles have stings	
Tobacco plants produce nicotine	

10. (a) (i) *Any two from:*
- Volume of extract/solution/sample
- pH (of solutions)
- time left in colorimeter/out of water bath

(ii) Shows what would happen without the lead ethanoate
OR that lead ethanoate is causing the effect/inhibiting the enzyme

(b) Some reaction occurred immediately
OR Enzyme started working before lead added
OR Browning occurred before reading taken
OR Pigment produced as soon as cut up

(c) (i) Appropriate enclosed scales with zeros and labels from table

(ii) Correct plots joined by straight lines and correct label from table

(d) As concentration increases, the activity (of the enzyme) decreases/effect of enzyme decreases/the enzyme is inhibited more

(e) Any figure from 1·6 and less than 2·0
Enzyme has been denatured

11. (a) They share/have a common ancestor/the same ancestor/have evolved from a single species
AND different mouths/heads (shapes) for different food/feeding methods

(b) They would be unable to interbreed/breed together to produce fertile offspring
OR if they interbreed they produce sterile offspring

(c) (i) Ecological **OR** reproductive

(ii) Prevents gene/exchange/flow
OR prevents breeding between populations/sub-populations

12. (a) L

(b) Xylem

(c) Spring
xylem (cells) produced last were wider

13. (a) Regulator (gene)

(b) Lactose

(c) (i) 1. Repressor (molecule) binds to/attaches/binds/joins with/blocks operator
2. Operator switches off structural gene
3. Enzyme/(β) galactosidase not made

(ii) Saves energy/ATP/resources

14. (a) (i) Iron needed for haemoglobin
AND haemoglobin carries oxygen (to tissues)

(ii) Reduced/retarded/stunted growth
OR low birthweight
AND reduced mental development

(b) (i) Decreasing photoperiod/description of decreasing photoperiod

(ii) Offspring born in spring/summer when weather/food supply more favourable

15. (a) Succession

(b) Makes soil more fertile/deeper/thicker
OR soil has more nutrients/minerals/ions/humus/organic matter
OR soil has better drainage/more aeration/better water retention

(c) Greater than
Community Y (both needed)

Section C

1A *Any four points from the following:*

(i) 1. contains protein
2. contains phospholipid
3. bilayer/double layer/two layers of phospholipids
4. phospholipids are fluid/constantly moving
5. protein arranged as a mosaic/patchy pattern/scattered/interspersed
5a. fluid mosaic pattern/model **(only award if 4 or 5 not scored)**
6. has channel forming proteins/pores

Any three points from the following:

(ii) 7. carriers/bind ions/molecules/proteins
AND move/carry/them across membrane
8. ion/molecule uptake is selective **OR** description
9. low to high concentration **OR** against concentration gradient
10. requires energy/ATP

Any three points from the following

(iii) 11. made of cellulose fibres
12. fully/freely permeable
13. provides support/rigidity for cells/plants **OR** gives cell shape
14. stops cells bursting after water uptake/when turgid/when placed in hypotonic solution

1B (i) *Any six points from the following:*
1. double helix
2. two chains/strands of nucleotides
3. deoxyribose sugar, phosphate and base make up a nucleotide
4. nucleotides joined together by sugar - phosphates bonds
OR sugar and phosphate joined to form backbones/chains/strands
5. base names (all four)
6. complementary bases pair
7. (weak) hydrogen bonding between bases

Any three points from the following:

(ii) 8. the molecule unwinds/uncoils/untwists **AND** unzips/H bonds between bases break
9. base pairing of (free) DNA nucleotides with complementary partners
10. sugar-phosphate bonds/backbones form
11. rewinds into two double helices **OR** two double helices form
12. requires enzymes **OR** ATP

Any one point from:
13. identical OR exactly the same DNA/molecules/copies produced
14. ensures daughter/new cells have complete/correct/the same genetic information

2A *Any four points from the following:*
1. nitrogen for amino acid/protein/enzymes
2. nitrogen for bases of nucleic acids/DNA/RNA/nucleotides
3. nitrogen for chlorophyll
   OR plant deficient in nitrogen will not have any chlorophyll
4. phosphorus for nucleic acids/DNA/RNA/RuBP/NADP/GP/ATP
5. magnesium for chlorophyll **OR** plant deficient in magnesium will not have any chlorophyll

Any four points from:
6. nitrogen deficiency produces chlorosis/yellow leaves/pale green leaves
7. nitrogen deficiency produces red leaf bases
8. nitrogen deficiency produces long roots
9. phosphorus deficiency produces red leaf bases
10. magnesium deficiency produces chlorosis
11. nitrogen/phosphorus/magnesium deficiency stunts/reduces/retards/restricts growth

Coherence
- divided into clear sections (including tabulation)
- must be 5 points in total
- At least 2/3 points on use of elements and at least 2/3 points on deficiency symptoms
- Total of three points required

Relevance
- no mention of other elements eg potassium or effects of light eg etiolation
- must be 5 points in total
- At least 2/3 points on use of elements and at least 2/3 points on deficiency symptoms
- Total of three points required

2B *Any two points from the following:*
1. they include disease/parasites, food supply/lack of food/competition for food, predation, competition for space/territory/shelter, toxic waste produced by organisms (any 2)
2. a third factor

And four points from:
3. increasing population/number of animals intensifies/increases the effect of density-dependent factors (or converse)
4. at higher pops – more/easier spread of disease/parasites
5. – less food available/more competition for food
6. – more predation/predators
7. – more competition for space/territory/shelter
8. – more toxic wastes from organism
9. this reduces population
10. reduced effect of factor allows population to rise again
11. result is that populations/numbers remain stable/are regulated

And two points from:
12. include temperature/rainfall/natural events eg flood/fire/earthquake/drought/rain storm/desertification/deforestation (any 2)
13. increasing population size does not intensify/increase the effect of density-independent factors

14. can cause extreme changes to population sizes

Coherence
- divided into clear sections
- At least 4 points on density dependent
- And at least 1 point on density independent
- Total of five points required

Relevance
- no mention of eg monitoring populations or conservation
- At least 4 points on density dependent
- And at least 1 point on density independent
- Total of five points required

HIGHER BIOLOGY 2010

Section A

1.	D	16.	C
2.	B	17.	D
3.	C	18.	D
4.	B	19.	A
5.	C	20.	B
6.	D	21.	C
7.	A	22.	C
8.	D	23.	A
9.	D	24.	D
10.	D	25.	A
11.	A	26.	B
12.	B	27.	C
13.	C	28.	A
14.	B	29.	C
15.	B	30.	A

Section B

1. (*a*) Protein, phospholipids, porous, selectively

(*b*) (i) 46.5 units (+/- 0.5)
(ii) 800 µg per hour
(iii)
1. Respiration provides the energy/for uptake/
ATP   active
transport

2. Cyanide   reduces   respiration (enzymes)
inhibits/   energy/ATP release
stops/
prevents

3. (More) cyanide   gives decreased   uptake/
prevents/stops   active
transport

or

Less energy/ATP   gives decreased   uptake/
prevents/stops   active
transport

2. (*a*) (On surface of/in/on) grana/granum

(*b*) Species – B
Explanation:
More   accessory pigment/
Higher mass of   carotene and xanthophyll
allows absorption of light   transmitted/ reflected (by other
plants)
not absorbed (by other plants)

(*c*) (i) A – carbon dioxide/CO_2
B – glucose/carbohydrate
(ii) Reduces/reduction of GP/CO_2
(iii) RuBP 5
GP 3
(iv) RuBP   decrease
GP   increase/more/accumulates
Explanation: No/less ATP/NADPH available

3. (*a*) (i) 7.5 grams per litre
(ii) 0.2 grams per litre per minute

(*b*) (i) 1. Anaerobic respiration   produces ethanol
Anaerobic conditions
Fermentation
2. Oxygen (in air)   starts aerobic respiration/
stops anaerobic respiration/
stops fermentation
(ii) The ethanol   has poisoned/   the yeast
Concentration   killed/become
lethal to

or

all glucose/food/respiratory substrate used up

4. (*a*) (i) X – deoxyribose
Y – phosphate
(ii) 1. cytosine/C
2. thymine/T
(iii) Enzyme(s) **or** (DNA) polymerase = **1**
ATP = **1**
(iv) Cell division **or** mitosis **or** meiosis

(*b*) TAG

5. (*a*) (i) Lymphocytes
(ii) (foreign) antigen

(*b*) (i) 1 : 3 : 4
(ii) Black
(iii) The more tannin /the greater the tannin content the
less fungus/leaf area covered
or use values from the table
(iv) (Fresh mass includes) water which can
change/vary/fluctuate

6. (*a*) (i) (As distance increases) from 500 to 2500m the number
of dances decreases from 6 to 3/falls by 3 = **1**
(when distance increased) from 2500 to 5000m the
number decreased from 3 to 2/falls by 1 = **1**
or (500 m to 5000m dances drop from 6 to 2) = **1**
(ii) 1.25s
(iii) 500%
(iv) 6s

(*b*) (i) 2.5
(ii) 3500m

(*c*) (i) Direction **or** quantity **or** quality (of food)
(ii) Reduces/saves the energy spent in foraging/ finding
food
or ensures a net energy gain **or** description of net
energy gain
or conserves energy by going straight to food source

7. (*a*) Same genes/sequence of genes/order of genes
or genes match gene for gene

(*b*) (i) Chiasma(ta)
(ii) Increases   variation
or
Allows   new combinations of alleles

(*c*) (i) Abcd P only
aBCD P only
AbcD P and Q
aBCd P and Q
(ii) abcD **or** ABCd **or** reverses

8. (*a*) (i) Affected female $X^R X^R$ and $X^R X^r$
Unaffected female $X^r X^r$ = **1**
(ii) 50%
(iii) Substitution
One amino acid altered

(*b*) Promotes the absorption/uptake of <u>calcium</u> from the
intestine

9. (a) Problem
   lose water by osmosis
   or cells/tissue/fish hypotonic to sea/surroundings
   or sea/surroundings hypertonic to cells/tissue/fish
   or higher water concentration in fish than sea/surroundings
   Fish Physiological
   chloride secretory cells secrete/get rid of salt/ions
   or (kidney with) few/small glomeruli
   or low kidney filtration rate
   or slow kidney filtration
   Rat Behavioural
   Nocturnal/active/feeds at night
   or remain in burrow by day
   Rat Physiological
   • no sweat glands/sweating
   • colon/large intestine efficient at absorbing water
   • long loops of Henle **or** kidney tubules allow high reabsorption of water
   • high level of ADH

   (b) Allow leaf/plant to float **or** make it buoyant **or** prevent it sinking **or** keeps it at the surface
   and To keep it in light for photosynthesis
   or To allow gas exchange through the stomata

10. (a) (i) Diameter/size/mass/number/surface area of beads **or** type of gel **or** time tap kept open **or** strain/concentration/mass/batch of *E.coli*
      or same volume of solution collected
      (ii) Same/identical funnel with gel beads without *E. Coli*
      To show *E.coli* produced the enzyme/ lactose did not beak down alone/ *E.coli* is the factor affecting lactose/ lactose is broken down by β galactosidase

   (b) Scales and labels = **1**
   Plots and line = **1**

   (c) 0.04 grams per minute

   (d) *Any two from:*
   Repressor joins with lactose/inducer
   or Operator switches on structural gene
   or Structural gene produces enzyme/ β galactosidase
   or Time needed to breakdown lactose
   or
   Enzyme being induced/produced/made/released = **1**
   Time needed to breakdown lactose = **1**

   (e) Saves/does not waste energy/ATP
   or saves/does not waste resources

11. (a) (i) 3-4 weeks and 4-5 weeks
      (ii) A
      (iii) Photosynthesis
      (iv) Dispersal of seeds/fruits **or** decomposition

   (b) length/thickness/width of stem/shoots/roots/ internodes
   or height/length of plant
   or number of leaves

   (c) (Apical) meristem

12. (a) Gene mutation
   (b) Gain tyrosine from diet/food
   and can be converted to pigment/ enzyme 3 still working/present
   (c) controls metabolic rate/metabolism

13. (a) B – Nitrogen   protein (synthesis)/enzymes/ amino acids/nucleic acids/ RNA/DNA/ATP/chlorophyll/ NAD/NADP
   C – Magnesium

   (b) Term – Etiolated/etiolation
   Long stems/internodes
   or yellow/pale/small/curled/chlorotic leaves

14. (a) (i) 22.5 **or** 23 beetles per m^2
      (ii) Food (supply) **or** predators **or** disease
      or competition for food/space
      Rainfall/drought/flooding **or** temperature **or** pesticide/insecticide **or** named natural disaster eg (forest) fire

   (b) *Any two from:*
   (Conservation/management of) endangered species
   (Conservation/management of) food species/source
   (Conservation/management of) raw material species/source
   Indicate levels of pollution

Section C

1A *Any six points from the following:*
   (i) 1. IAA Stimulates/promotes cell division/mitosis
        2. IAA Stimulates/promotes cell elongation
        3. IAA Stimulates/promotes differentiation
        4. IAA causes apical dominance/inhibits (growth of) lateral buds
        5. IAA is important/involved in tropic effects/ tropisms/geotropism/phototropism
        6. IAA causes shoot/plant growth towards light **or** description
        7. Low/fall in/decrease in IAA (concentration) causes abscission/leaf fall **or** converse
        8. IAA causes fruit formation/development/ growth

   Any four points from the following:
   (ii) 9. GA produced in embryo
        10. GA travels to aleurone layer
        11. GA stimulates/induces/switches on gene for production of (α-)amylase in aleurone layer
        12. (α-)amylase breaks down/digests starch to maltose
        13. maltose required for respiration/ATP production
        14. GA breaks dormancy (of seeds)

1B *Any two points from the following:*
   (i) 1. endotherms can regulate/control/maintain their (body) temperature (physiologically)
        and ectotherms cannot/ectotherms temperature is dependent on their environment/behaviour
        2. endotherms derive (most body) heat from respiration/metabolism/chemical reactions
        3 ectotherms derive/get (body) heat from surroundings/environment **or** description of behaviour

   Any eight points from the following:
   (ii) 4. temperature monitoring centre/ thermoreceptors in hypothalamus
        5. nerve message sent to skin/effectors
        6. vasodilation/widening of blood vessels to skin in response to increased temperature
        or vasoconstriction/narrowing of blood vessels to skin in response to decreased temperature
        7. more/less blood to skin/extremities **or** less/more blood in body core
        8. increased/more **or** decreased/less heat radiated from skin/extremities
        9. increased temperature leads to (increase in) sweat production **or** converse
        10. increase in heat loss due to evaporation of (water in) sweat **or** converse
        11. Decrease in temperature causes hair erector muscles to raise/erect hair

12. traps (warm) air **or** forms insulating layer
13. Decrease in temperature causes muscle contraction/shivering which generates heat/raises body temperature
14. temperature regulation involves/is an example of negative feedback

2A *Any two points from the following:*
1. isolating mechanisms prevent gene flow between (sub-) populations/groups **or**
   isolating mechanisms are barriers to gene exchange between/breeding between\mutations being passed between
   or isolating mechanisms split a gene pool
2. geographic, ecological, reproductive (any two)
3. third

Any two points from:
4. mutations occur randomly
5. different mutations occur in each (sub-) population/group
6. Mutations increase/decrease survival
   or mutations can be beneficial
   or mutations can provide a selective advantage

Any two points from:
7. different conditions/habitat/environment exist for each (sub-)population
8. natural selection acts differently on/there are different selection pressures on each (sub-)population/groups
9. surviving/best suited/fittest individuals are able to breed/pass on (favourable) genes/alleles/mutations
10. over long periods after many generations
11. new species formed/speciation has occurred
12. new species are unable to interbreed/breed together to produce fertile young

Coherence
* divided into 3 clear sections
* At least 1/2 points on isolation (Points 1 – 3)
* At least 1/2 points on mutation (Points 4 – 6)
* And at least 2/3 points on natural selection (Points 7 – 12)
* total of five points required

Relevance
* no mention of artificial selection
* At least 1/2 points on isolation (Points 1 – 3)
* And at least 1/2 points on mutation (Points 4 – 6)
* And at least 2/3 points on natural selection (Points 7 – 12)
* total of five points required

2B *Any six points from the following:*
1. water moves into root (hair cells)by osmosis/from HWC to LWC/down water concentration gradient
2. water moves across/enters the cortex by osmosis/from HWC to LWC/down water concentration gradient
3. water enters xylem
4. water moves through xylem(vessels)
5. cohesion is attraction between/sticking together of water molecules
6. adhesion is attraction between water (molecules) and xylem (walls)/sticking of water molecules to xylem
5a. adhesion and cohesion named (if neither 5 nor 6 is scored)
7. water moves into leaf cells by osmosis/from HWC to LWC /down a water concentration gradient
8. water evaporates into (leaf) air spaces
9. water vapour diffuses from leaf surfaces/ lost through stomata

Any two points from:
10. water (provides raw material) for photosynthesis/photolysis
11. water provides turgidity/keeps cells turgid
12. causes cooling/cools the plant
13. minerals/nutrients/ions supplied/transported

Coherence
* Divided into clear sections
* At least 4 points on transpiration stream (Points 1 – 9)
* And at least 1 point on importance (Points 10 – 13)
* total of five points required

Relevance
* No mention of details of xerophytes or hydrophytes, mineral deficiencies
* At least 4 points on transpiration stream (Points 1 – 9)
* And at least 1 point on importance (Points 10 – 13)
* total of five points required

HIGHER BIOLOGY 2011

Section A

1.	C	16.	C
2.	A	17.	B
3.	C	18.	A
4.	D	19.	B
5.	B	20.	C
6.	D	21.	C
7.	C	22.	D
8.	A	23.	A
9.	A	24.	B
10.	D	25.	B
11.	B	26.	C
12.	B	27.	D
13.	D	28.	C
14.	D	29.	A
15.	A	30.	D

Section B

1. (a) P mitochondrion/mitochondria

    Q (cavity of) Golgi (apparatus/body)
    or smooth ER

   (b) (i) 1. Protein
        2. Phospholipid (either way round)

      (ii) Selectively/semi permeable
        or description based on comparison of molecular size

   (c) Hypotonic

   (d) 1. Draws food/particles/micro-organisms in using cilia
        or moves to food/particles/microorganism using cilia

      2. Encloses   food   into a (food) vacuole/vesicle
         Engulfs   particles
         Seals in   micro-organisms
         or endocytosis

      3. Lysosomes fuse with/attach to (food) vacuole
      4. Digests   food   with enzymes from lysosomes
         Breaks down   particles

2. (a) Cytoplasm

   (b) Enzymes **or** ATP **or** ADP **or** NAD **or** Pi

   (c) R pyruvic acid/pyruvate
       S ethanol/alcohol

   (d) Oxygen needed as a final/last/terminal acceptor of hydrogen

3. (a) 1440

   (b) Oxygen is no longer limiting/a limiting factor
       or
       Another factor/temp/glucose/respiratory substrate is limiting
       or
       ATP production/aerobic respiration has reached the maximum
       or potassium uptake is at its maximum

   (c) 1. Enzyme activity less/now reduced
        or 20°C/temp/conditions not optimum for enzymes/ below optimum for enzymes
      2. ATP production/respiration requires enzymes
        or mention of respiratory enzymes
      3. Less energy/ATP available/released/produced
      4. Active uptake/transport requires energy
        or potassium upake is active/requires energy

4. (a) (i) Photosynthesis occurs in wavelengths/colours of light/ green/yellow light/regions of spectrum little absorbed by the pigment/pigment shown/ chlorophyll
        or Photosynthesis occurs when absorption of green/yellow/by the pigment is low
        or Photosynthesis occurs in all colours but the pigment absorbs mainly blue and red/little yellow/ green (light)

      (ii) (Paper/thin layer) chromatography

   (b) 1. Photosynthesis occurs in red and blue light
      2. Photosynthesis produces oxygen
      3. (Aerobic) bacteria go to areas where oxygen is most abundant

5. (a) (i)

	X^R	X^r
X^r	X^{R}X^r	X^{r}X^r
Y	X^{R}Y	X^{r}Y

      (ii) All boxes ticked

      (iii) Fertilisation/Fusion of gametes is a random/chance process
        or sample size/offspring number too small

   (b) NKML **or** LMKN

6. (a) (i) 1. From 0 to 5 days/for the first 5 days it remains constant/stays at 1375 units
        2. From 5 to 15 days/next 10 days drops to 450 units/falls by 925 units
        3. **or** From 15 to 25 days/for next 10 days/for remaining days stays constant at 450 units

      (ii) 60

      (iii) 50

      (iv) It would never reach its compensation point
        or Compensation point greater than 400 (units)
        or Lowest compensation point is 500 (units)
        or Compensation point levels off at 500 (units)
        or Needs more than/at least 500 (units) to grow

        No net energy gain
        or respiration would exceed photosynthesis
        or more carbohydrate/glucose/food used than gained

   (b) (i) Spider plant
        Reason Spider plant has compensation points of 250 units at day 20 and/or 500 units at day 10 in Graph 1/ the other Graph
        or
        The compensation points (in Graph 2) match compensation point in Graph 1

      (ii) 1.75 times

7. (a) (i) AUG

      (ii) Second base is G/guanine
        or guanine in second/centre position
        or contains guanine
        or None have uracil/U

   (b) Isoleucine, glutamine

8. (a) Radiation/example of radiation

   (b) (i) Insertion
           Deletion
           Substitution
           Inversion

      (ii) Gene mutation numbers 1 and 2

           Explanation:
           Will affect many codons/triplets/amino acids
           or
           They will affect every codon/triplet/amino acid after
           the mutation/from that point on

9. (a) (i) Bring down/kill larger prey
           or Increases hunting success/better chance of catching
           prey
           or Less energy expended per individual
           or Greater net gain of energy per individual

           Reduces/less (inter/intra) competition

      (ii) Ensures that energy gained in food is greater than energy
           expended in catching food/hunting food/ foraging
           or converse

     (iii) Numbers confuse the predator/lion
           or Individuals take turns at watching for predators/lions
           or More chance that at least one individual will see
           predator/lion
           or More chance of spotting/getting warning about
           predator/lion
           or Description of group protection in wildebeest
           or Harder to single out individual

   (b) (i) Avoidance (behaviour)

      (ii) Reduces chances of being eaten
           or reduces predation
           or Protection from predators

10. (a) Temperature **or** variety/type/species/age of rice (grains)

   (b) (i) Shows that it is GA which is causing the
           results/germination/breaking of dormancy
           or shows results without GA to compare to
           others/those with GA

      (ii) Some GA is already present in (rice) grains/seeds/
           embryo
           or (rice) grains/seeds/embryo produces GA

   (c) Use of 50 (rice) grains at each concentration/each time/in
       each solution/in each beaker

   (d) Increased
       Reason   evaporation of water/solvent

   (e) 42

(f) Scales – both need 0s, at least half grid used

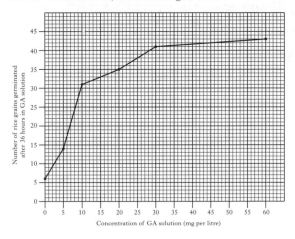

Labels – from table
Plot – accurate plots and straight lines

(g) 1. Increasing GA concentration increases
        germination/number germinating
        or increasing GA concentration above 30 mg per litre
        has little effect on rate of germination
        or between 5 and 10 mg per litre of GA greatest
        increase in germination/number germinated
    2. The longer in GA (solution) the greater
        germination/number germinating

(h) Aleurone (layer)

11. (a) A and B
        moult   allows   increases in length
        exoskeleton/skin shed   is followed by   inflation
                                                 growth

        B and C
        exoskeleton/skin prevents increase in length
        or restricts/limits/inhibits growth

   (b) (i) X Growth hormone/GH/somatotrophin
           Y Thyroid stimulating hormone/TSH

      (ii) Thyroid

     (iii) Controls/increases/regulates/stimulates the metabolic
           rate/metabolism/metabolic processes

12. (a) (i) As galactosidase/enzyme increases/is
            produced/appears/is introduced the lactose decreases
            or lactose begins to fall/decrease after galactosidase
            levels increase/starts to be produced

       (ii) True
            False
            True

   (b) Undifferentiated
       Genes
       Limited

13. (a) H
        B F
        B D
        A

   (b) E, A

14. (a) Hypothalamus   – B/water and C/temperature
        Pancreas   – A/glucose

   (b) 1. Glucagon
       2. Adrenaline/epinephrine

(*c*) Decrease the permeability (of kidney tubule cells) to water

(*d*) (i) Vasoconstriction/constriction/narrowing of diameter

Less/inhibits/reduces blood flow to skin so less heat is lost by <u>radiation</u>

(ii) Endotherms

Section C

1A *Any six points from the following:*
(i) 1. fish (tissues) hypotonic to/at higher water concentration than sea water/surroundings/ environment **or** converse
2. water loss by osmosis through mouth/gills
3. drinks sea/salt water
4. chloride secretory cells in gills secrete/excrete/remove/ get rid of salt
5. by active transport/actively/against concentration gradient
6. (kidneys have) few small glomeruli
7. slow filtration/low rate of filtration
8. low volume/amount of concentrated urine

Any four points from the following:
(ii) 9. behavioural and physiological (mechanisms)
10. active by night/nocturnal **or** stays in (damp/humid) burrow by day
11. dry faeces **or** efficient absorption of water by large intestine
12 does not sweat/no sweat glands **or** dry mouth and nasal passages
13. long loops of Henle/kidney tubules so high/more/ increased reabsorption of water
or high/increased levels of ADH so high/more/ increased reabsorption water
14. low volumes/amounts of concentrated urine

1B *Any four points from the following:*
(i) 1. gamete mother cells (undergo meiosis)
2. spindle forms **or** nuclear membrane breaks down
3. homologous chromosomes pair
4. homologous chromosomes line up at equator/middle of cell
or crossing over occurs at chiasmata
5. homologous chromosomes segregate/move apart
or independent assortment occurs
6. Cytoplasm splits/new nuclear membranes form
7. two haploid cells/cells with one set of chromosomes/ cells with half the number of chromosomes form

Any three points from the following:
8. two new spindles form
9. chromosomes line up on equator/middle of cell
10. chromatids separate/are pulled apart
11. cytoplasm splits/new nuclear membranes form
12. to give four haploid cells/gametes

Any three points from the following:
(ii) 13. Independent/random assortment **or** description of independent assortment
14. crossing over
15. recombination **or** description of recombination
16. non-disjunction/description

2A *Any six from the following:*
1. occurs in stroma of chloroplasts
2. carbon dioxide/CO_2 accepted by RuBP to produce GP/PGA
3. glucose C6, RuBP 5C and GP/PGA 3C
4. NADP carries/supplies hydrogen to Calvin cycle/ carbon fixation stage
5. H/H2/Hydrogen reduces GP/PGA/carbon dioxide/ CO2 to glucose/carbohydrate
6. ATP provides energy
7. GP/PGA used to regenerate/make/generate/produce RuBP
8. enzyme controlled/requires enzymes

Any two from the following:
9. energy in carbohydrate/glucose
or produces glucose for respiration
10. produces cellulose **or** structural carbohydrate **or** carbohydrate for cell walls
11. produces storage carbohydrate **or** starch
12. major biological molecules **or** protein, fat, lipid, nucleic acid, nucleotides are derived/produced/ made

Coherence
• Divided into clear sections
• At least 3/4 points on carbon fixation
• And at least 1/2 points on significance
• *Total of five points required*

Reference
• No mention of details of light dependent stage other than ATP/NADPH supplied by this stage
• At least 3/4 points on carbon fixation
• And at least 1/2 points on significance
• *Total of five points required*

2B *Any five points from the following:*
1. virus attaches stick/joins/adheres to (host) cell
2. viral nucleic acid/DNA/RNA/virus enters/injected in
3. viral nucleic acid/DNA/RNA/virus takes over/alters cell metabolism
or viral nucleic acid/DNA/RNA/virus alters cell instructions
4. viral nucleic acid/DNA/RNA replicated
5. protein coats synthesised/produced
6. (host) cell supplies nucleotides/enzymes/ATP/amino acids
7. (new) viruses assembled/or description
8. (new) viruses released by (host) cell bursting/lysis

Any three from the following:
9. lymphocytes produce antibodies
10. antibodies produced in response to foreign/non-self antigens
11. antibodies are specific to antigens
12. antibodies destroy/render harmless/inactivate antigens/viruses/bacteria/pathogens

Coherence
• Divided into clear sections
• At least 3 points on viruses
• And at least 2 points on lymphocytes
• *Total of five points required*

Reference
• No mention of details of replication/protein synthesis/ phagocytes
• At least 3 points on viruses
• And at least 2 points on lymphocytes
• *Total of five points required*

HIGHER BIOLOGY 2012

Section A

1.	B	16.	A
2.	A	17.	B
3.	A	18.	B
4.	D	19.	C
5.	A	20.	B
6.	B	21.	B
7.	C	22.	C
8.	C	23.	A
9.	D	24.	D
10.	D	25.	B
11.	C	26.	D
12.	C	27.	C
13.	D	28.	D
14.	A	29.	A
15.	B	30.	C

Section B

1. (a) (i) P stroma

   (ii) Grana/granum/thylakoids
   absent/destroyed/removed/disappeared/disintegrated/
   broken down/dissolved/gone
   or no grana

   (iii) 1. ATP
   2. NADPH/NADPH$_2$/hydrogen/H/H$_2$

   (b) Less CO$_2$ to combine with/convert/change/join to/bind to RuBP
   or less RuBP is converted into GP/TP/6C compound/
   Glucose/carbohydrate

   GP/TP changed/converted/regenerated to RuBP

2. (a) TACATCATG or GTACTACAT

   (b) Ribosome

   (c) AUC

   (d) Peptide

3. (a) Solution hypotonic/less concentrated/had a higher water concentration (than tissue)
   or
   Tulip/plant/stem/cells hypertonic/more concentrated/had a lower water concentration (than solution)
   and
   Water enters/passes into tulip/plant/stem/cells (by osmosis)

   (b) 0.45

   (c) Plasmolysed/ Flaccid

4. (a) Allow respiration of snail to become steady
   or
   Allow snail to adjust/get used to conditions/temperature/ surroundings/environment
   or
   allow snail to acclimatise
   or
   Allow pressures to equalise
   or
   Allow liquid levels to settle/become zero (at 20°C)

(b) Same /apparatus/experiment/set-up/procedure /but with no snail/glass beads/dead snail

(c) Volume/concentration of solution (to absorb carbon dioxide)
or
Diameter/width of glass tube/scale
or
(Same) snail/mass of snail/species/type of snail/size of snail

(d)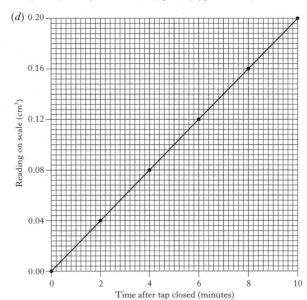

(e) 0.004
or
4×10^{-3}

(f) Oxygen taken in by snail/used in respiration causes the liquid to rise/move/go up
or
As the snail respires, oxygen level falls causing liquid to rise/move/go up (1)
CO$_2$ produced by snail/respiration is absorbed/taken in by/removed by the solution (1)
or
Oxygen taken in by snail/used in respiration and CO$_2$ produced by snail/respiration absorbed by solution (1)
Volume of gas/pressure decreases and liquid moves/rises (1)

5. (a) (i) The warmer/hotter the zone/climate the greater the % (of cyanogenic clover)
or
As temperature increases, the % (of cyanogenic clover plants) increases
or
Converse

   (ii) Increased/more/greater % cyanogenic plants giving protection against herbivores/prevents/reduces grazing by herbivores /damage by herbivores
or
Converse
or
Increased/more/greater % cyanogenic plant in areas where non-cyanogenic plants have been removed/ eaten by herbivores
or
Increased/more/greater % cyanogenic plants where they have a selective advantage

   (iii) Nicotine/tannin

(iv) Low/underground meristems
deep roots/rhizomes/underground stems/underground food stores/bulbs/tubers/corms

(b) Resin

6. (a) 1. The greater the distance from cover of the prey/ redshanks/birds the lower the (hunting) success/ number caught/number killed
or
2. The greater the flock size/number of redshank/birds the lower the hunting success /number caught/number killed
or
Converses

(b) (i) Avoidance

(ii) Habituation/habituated

7. (a) (i) Ovary
or
Anther/stamen

(ii) First

Homologous pairs/homologous chromosomes/bivalent separating/present/being pulled apart/lined up

(iii) Gamete: 4
Mother cell: 8

(b) (i) Crossing over/recombination
or
Random assortment
or
Independent assortment

(ii) Non-disjunction

8. (a) (i) aabb (any order)
Cushion
AB, Ab, aB, ab (any order)

(ii) 1:1:1:1

(b) Linked/linkage

9. (a) Hypertonic, into

(b) Increase until day 9/until 615 <u>micrometres</u>/by 335 <u>micrometres</u>/for 4 days (1)
Then remains the same/levels out/shows no change (1)

(c)

Kidney function	Increases	Decreases	Stays the same
Filtration rate	✓		
Urine concentration		✓	
Urine volume	✓		

10. (a) (i) 1. Rate drops from 180 to 150cm^3/m^2/hr from 0 to 10mg/l
2. Remains constant at 150cm^3/m^2/hr between 10 and 20 mg/l
3. Drops from 150 to 100cm^3/m^2/hr from 20 to 40 mg/l/over the next 20mg/l

(ii) Decrease (in transpiration rate) is not steady as lead concentration increases
or
Graph is not a straight line/levels off between 10 and 20mg/l
or
Between 10 and 20 mg/l /there is no change/stays the same

(b) 60% decrease

(c) (i) 0.04 mg per g dry mass

(ii) 40 : 1

(d) Moisture/water content of/in fresh mass/shoots/roots/ plants varies/fluctuates/changes/is different in each plant

(e) 50mg lead

(f) Lead inhibits/slows down enzymes (1)
Less respiration/ATP/energy/protein synthesis/ photosynthesis/DNA replication/cell division/mitosis (1)

11. (a) (i) 5.5 kg

(ii) 1–5 years

(b) (i) Hormone W – TSH/thyroid stimulating hormone
Hormone X – GH/growth hormone/somatotrophin
Structure Y – Thyroid (gland)

(ii) Increase in/speeds up metabolism/metabolic rate

12. (a) (i) 1. Stimulates/promotes/increases (cell) division/elongation/mitosis/vacuolation
2. Apical dominance

(ii) Some genes are switched/turned on and others are switched/turned off
or
Only certain/specific/particular genes are switched/turned on
or
Different genes are switched on/off in different cell types

(b) (i) Component of chlorophyll

(ii) Red leaf bases

13. (a) (i) Hypothalamus

(ii) Nerves/nerve impulses/nerve messages/nerve signals

(iii) Example – increased sweating **or** vasodilation
Explanation – heat lost/skin cools as sweat/water evaporates
or
Increased heat loss by radiation

(iv) Metabolism/metabolic processes controlled by enzymes **and** enzymes have an optimum temperature/ a temperature at which they work best

(b) Ectotherm

14. (a) (i) Prey increases as predators numbers are/predation is low/decreasing (1)
Then prey decreases as predator numbers are/ predation is high/increasing (1)

(ii) Food supply/availability **or** competition for food **or** disease/parasites **or** competition for space/habitat **or** toxic waste builds up/accumulates **or** toxic waste produced by organism

(b) Food/raw materials
Control (of the pest species)/limit damage /keep pest numbers low/limits spread of disease/show if pest control is effective/shows if pesticide was effective
Indicator
Conservation/protection **or** prevent extinction **or** maintain/prevent decline of population

15. (a) (i) 1. Long
Twelve

(ii) 2. Will not flower
Needs 14 hours continuous/uninterrupted dark (to flower)
or needs 10 hours or less of light (to flower)

(b) (i) Spring
Young born when weather (eg of favourable weather)/food supply better
or
Gives time for growth/development before winter

(ii) Photoperiodism

Section C

1A *Any six points from the following:*

(i) 1. isolation prevents interbreeding/mating or genes/alleles/mutations flowing/being exchanged between one group/(sub) population and another
or
isolation splits the gene pool

2. isolation/barrier can be geographical/ecological/reproductive (*Any two*)

3. a third barrier

4. mutations are random

5. mutations can be beneficial (or not)/give (selective) advantage (or not)

6. mutations are different in different groups/(sub) populations

7. environments/conditions/habitats/surroundings different on either side of the barrier
or
environments/conditions/habitats/surroundings of each population differ

8. selection pressure(s) are different on either side of the barrier
or
selection pressure(s) on each population differ

Any four points from the following:

(ii) 9. survival of the fittest/those with the most favourable/beneficial characteristics/genes/alleles/phenotypes/mutations/the best suited to the environment

10. (survive to) pass on favourable/beneficial characteristics/genes/alleles/phenotypes/ mutations to offspring

11. adaptive radiation

12. after long periods of time/many generations

13. new species are formed/speciation occurs

14. populations would be unable to breed with each other/interbreed to produce fertile young/offspring

1B *Any two points from the following:*

(i) 1. foraging is searching for/obtaining/hunting for food/prey

2. net gain of energy
or
energy gain in food/prey must be greater than that lost in foraging/ searching for food/obtaining food/hunting
or Converse

3. behaviour/search pattern is organised to minimise energy loss or maximise energy gain

Any seven points from the following:

(ii) 4. hunting together/working together/working as a team to obtain food/prey

5. increases success rate
or
more chance of catching prey

6. large/larger prey obtained/caught/killed

7. less energy used/lost per individual
or
more energy/food gained per individual

8. sharing occurs
or aggression is reduced
or all feed

9. dominance hierarchy is a pecking order/rank order/rank system
or some are dominant and some are subordinate

10. dominant/leader/alpha/highest ranking/highest in hierarchy eat first/get more/best food
or ensure survival of dominant/leader/alpha/highest ranking/highest in hierarchy when food scarce

11. <u>subordinate</u> gain more than by hunting alone

Any one point from the following:

12. territory is an area defended/marked for food
or energy is expended to defend/mark territory

13. territorial behaviour reduces competition for food

14. size of territory depends on food availability/density/abundance

2A *Any three points from the following:*

1. double membrane
or inner and outer membrane
or labelled diagram

2. central matrix
or fluid-filled matrix
or labelled diagram

3. matrix contains enzymes

4. cristae are folds in the inner membrane
or cristae have a large surface area
or labelled diagram

Any five points from the following:

5. cytochrome system/molecules/carriers on/in cristae

6. consists of hydrogen carriers/ hydrogen acceptors/electron transfer system/electron transport system

7. NAD/FAD/NADH/FADH/NADH$_2$/FADH$_2$ carries hydrogen to cristae/cytochrome system/electron transfer system/electron transport system

8. Iron required for/ is a component of cytochrome/cytochrome system/hydrogen carrier system

9. oxygen is the <u>final hydrogen acceptor</u>

10. water is produced

11. ATP is produced/synthesised/regenerated
or ADP + Pi → ATP

12. greatest source of ATP **or** most ATP produced (per glucose molecule respired)

Coherence

- Divided into clear sections
- At least 1 point on mitochondria structure
- And at least 4 points on cytochrome system
- *Total of five points required*

Relevance

- No mention of **details** of any other organelle or reactions
- At least 1 point on mitochondria structure
- And at least 4 points on cytochrome system
- *Total of five points required*

2B *Any four points from the following:*
1. phagocytosis is not specific/non-specific
2. carried out by phagocytes/phagocytic cells/macrophages
3. engulf/envelope/surround bacteria/viruses/foreign organisms/foreign cells/pathogens/antigens
4. vacuole/vesicle formed **or** enclosed in vacuole **or** diagram
5. lysosomes fuse/join with vacuole/vesicle
6. lysosomes contain/release digestive enzymes which destroy/digest/break down bacteria/viruses/foreign organisms/pathogens/antigens

Any four points from the following:
7. lymphocytes produce antibodies
8. antibody production is stimulated by/caused by/in response to foreign/non-self antigens
9. antibody production/response/antibody/action of lymphocytes is specific
10. antibodies combine with/join to antigens
11. bacteria/viruses/foreign organisms/foreign cells/pathogens/antigens rendered harmless/destroyed/agglutinated/broken down
12. involved in immunity/immune response

Coherence
- Divided into clear sections
- At least 2/3 points on phagocytosis
- And at least 2/3 points on lymphocytes
- *Total of five points required*

Relevance
- No mention of **details** of viruses
- At least 2/3 points on phagocytosis
- And at least 2/3 points on lymphocytes
- *Total of five points required*

HIGHER BIOLOGY 2013

Section A

1.	A	16.	B
2.	B	17.	C
3.	D	18.	A
4.	A	19.	C
5.	D	20.	D
6.	B	21.	D
7.	D	22.	B
8.	A	23.	A
9.	B	24.	C
10.	D	25.	B
11.	C	26.	A
12.	C	27.	B
13.	C	28.	C
14.	D	29.	B
15.	A	30.	C

Section B

1. (a) (i) X (inorganic) phosphate (group)
        Y deoxyribose (sugar)
      (ii) Z hydrogen/H

   (b) (i) *Any one from:*
        Step 2 bonds between bases/strands/nucleotides break
        or hydrogen bonds break
        or DNA (molecule) unzips
        or strands separate
        AND *any one from:*
        Step 4 sugar phosphate bonds/backbones form (between nucleotides)
        or bonds form between adjacent/neighbouring nucleotides
        or bonds form between one nucleotide and the next
      (ii) Enzymes / (DNA) polymerase
        or ATP
      (iii) Ensures each cell has identical/copy of/a full set of DNA genetic information
        or ensures that no genetic information gets lost
        or ensures each (daughter) cell can produce all of its enzymes/proteins

2. (a) (i) More/increased greenfly damage/destroy/injure/attack/eat (leaves)
        More glycosides converted to cyanide
      (ii) Greenfly numbers increase/do not decrease even although cyanide is increasing/present/being produced/high
      (iii) 0·4
      (iv) 0·33

   (b) Isolates/seals/covers/forms a protective layer over/coats infected/damaged/injured/wounded area/tissue
       or prevents spread/entry of/further damage by microorganisms/bacteria/fungi/viruses/pathogens/infection/disease
       or acts as a barrier to micro-organisms/bacteria/fungi/viruses/pathogens/infection/disease

3. (*a*) Root hair (cell)
Large/increased/maximises surface (area)

 (*b*) Active transport
Supplies/produces/provides/gives/releases/makes ATP/
energy
or Site of ATP production

4. (*a*) (i) Concentration of glucose (solution)
or pH
or strain/type/species/variety/age of yeast
or concentration of yeast
(ii) Allow the flasks/solutions/glucose and lead to reach the
appropriate temperature **or** 20°C/the temperature of
the water bath
(iii) Allow the lead (nitrate) to diffuse into/be absorbed by
cells/yeast
or allows lead (nitrate) to have its effect on/inhibit
respiration
or allows lead (nitrate) to have its effect on/inhibit/
react with enzymes

 (*b*)
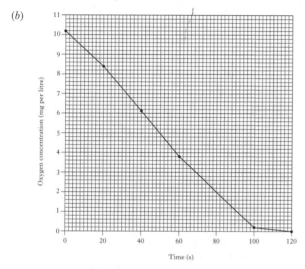

 (*c*) As the lead (concentration) increases respiration decreases
or inhibition was increased

 (*d*) (i) Carbon dioxide/CO_2
(ii) Anaerobic respiration/fermentation

5. (*a*) (i) RB, Rb, rB, rb
(ii)
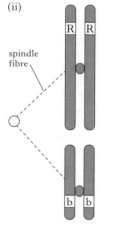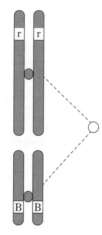

spindle
fibre

 (iii) Separation of chromatids

 (*b*) (i) Tick Eh and eH
(ii) Crossing over
Increases/causes/produces variation
or increases variety in offspring/gametes
or creates new phenotypes/genotypes/combinations of
alleles

6. (*a*) (i) Geographical
(ii) *Any one from:*
Prevents exchange of genes/alleles/mutations
or divides the gene pool
or prevents the gene pools mixing
or prevents populations/sub-populations/groups
breeding with each other
(iii) They would be unable to interbreed to produce fertile
offspring
or if they did interbreed they would produce infertile
offspring

 (*b*) (i) *Any one from:*
Gene probe/probing
chromosome banding/mapping
recombination frequency
Cross-over values
(ii) **Endonuclease**
Open/break open plasmid
or removing/separating/cutting gene/allele/DNA
from chromosome
or cut DNA
Ligase
Seals/sticks/glues/attaches/genes/alleles/DNA/into
plasmids
(iii) The blood clotting/human/gene has been inserted into
the tetracycline (resistance) gene
or the tetracycline (resistance) gene has been separated
/split/cut/interrupted
or sequence of bases on the tetracycline gene has been
interrupted
AND
Tetracycline (resistance) gene cannot be (fully)
transcribed/is not functional
or
protein which gives resistance cannot be translated/
produced

7. (*a*) **Q** $X^d Y$
S $X^D X^d$
W $X^D Y$

 (*b*) S is not affected but she inherits the allele/X^d/from Q/her
father
or S is $X^D X^d$/heterozygous/has both the dominant and
recessive allele/is a carrier but she is not affected
or V is affected but neither parent/R nor S was

 (*c*) *Any one from:*
Males inherit/one copy of the gene/allele so if it is
recessive/for red-green colour deficiency they will be
affected
females inherit two copies of the gene so could be carriers
females inherit two copies of the gene so have two chances
to inherit a dominant/masking allele
males need one recessive/red-green colour deficiency allele
to be affected but females need two

8. (*a*) (i) (curling) increases humidity/traps water vapour/
or (curling) creates still air conditions/reduces effect of
wind
or reduces surface area exposed AND reduces
transpiration/evaporation/diffusion of water vapour
(ii) uncurls/opens/unrolls
Larger surface area/more chloroplasts/more
chlorophyll to trap/absorb/take in light
or A larger surface area for CO_2 uptake/gas exchange
(iii) Xerophyte/xerophytic/xeromorphic

(b) **1** gives buoyancy/brings leaf to surface/helps leaf to float for photosynthesis/gas exchange
2 allows leaf to remain on surface when water level changes or prevents damage in water currents

9. (a) GA/gibberellic acid/gibberellin
embryo

(b) **Function** Converts/breaks down/digests starch to maltose/sugar
Importance Provides energy/ATP (for germination/mitosis)

10. (a) (i) **1** Increases from 4·0 - 4·5g to beginning of September/end of August
2 Falls from 4·5 – 1·5g from beginning of September/end of August until beginning of December/end of November.
3 Remains constant (at 1·5g) from beginning of December/end of November to end of January

(ii) 60%

(iii) *Any one from:*
More/plentiful/good food/nectar available
less energy needed to keep warm
more torpor than in winter
using less energy because not migrating

(b) (i) Energy conserved/saved for migration

(ii) (Conservation of) energy needed for breeding/courtship/nest building/feeding chicks/fighting for territory

(iii) 0·5

(c) 45cm³

(d) Reduces competition

11. (a) 2:3

(b) 3·5 hours

(c) **1** Glucose used in respiration/in glycolysis/to provide energy/to provide ATP
2 Glucose converted to/stored as/turned into glycogen
or glucose taken up by liver/muscle

(d) Increased
AND *any one from:*
Bring glucose back to normal/80mg per 100cm³
prevents glucose falling too low/further
keeps glucose levels normal/80mg per 100cm³

12. (a) (i) 0 – 2 years
(ii) X
(iii) (Body) mass increases when GH level falls/remains constant/remains steady

(b) Pituitary (gland)

13. (a) (i) **1** Lactose binds with repressor (molecule/protein)
2 Operator activates structural gene
3 Structural gene causes production of the enzyme/galactosidase **or** structural gene transcribed and translated

(ii) Saves/conserves/prevents waste of ATP/energy/resources/amino acids

(b) Add to each flask/solution
AND
It would turn yellow/change colour in Flask 1/where lactose was present **or** it would stay colourless in Flask 2/where lactose was absent

14. (a) Phototropism/phototropic
More light for photosynthesis
or grows towards light for photosynthesis

(b) (i) Substance/IAA/auxin accumulates on the dark side/side away from light
or less substance/IAA/auxin on light/unshaded side
or substance/IAA/auxin destroyed on the light side but not on the dark side
Elongation/mitosis/cell division on dark/shaded side/side away from light causing growth towards light

(ii) IAA/auxin/indole acetic acid

Section C

1A *Any four points from the following:*

(i) 1. pigments absorb light (energy)
2. light can be transmitted or reflected
3. chlorophyll absorbs (mainly) in the blue and red regions of the spectrum
or absorbs blue and red light
or absorbs red and blue wavelengths
4. accessory pigments/xanthophyll and carotene (and chlorophyll b)
absorb light from other regions of the spectrum/of other wavelengths/of other colours
or absorb green and yellow light
or absorb light/wavelengths/colours not absorbed by chlorophyll
or broaden/widen the absorption spectrum
5. accessory pigments/xanthophyll and carotene (and chlorophyll b) pass the energy (**NOT** light) on to chlorophyll
6. accessory pigments are xanthophyll, carotene (and chlorophyll b)
or all pigments named (chlorophyll a and b, xanthophyll, carotene)

Any six points from the following:

(ii) 7. (pigments/light dependent stage) in the grana
8. photolysis
9. water is split/broken down to release hydrogen and oxygen
10. hydrogen /carried by/joins with/attaches to NADP
or NADPH/NADPH₂ is made
11. NADPH/NADPH₂/ hydrogen needed for /transferred to carbon fixation stage/Calvin cycle **NOT** stroma/dark stage/light independent stage
12. oxygen released
or oxygen is a by-product/waste product
13. energy can be used in the regeneration/synthesis of ATP
or energy can be used in photophosphorylation
14. ATP is needed for /passed to the carbon fixation stage/Calvin cycle
NOT stroma/dark stage/light independent stage

1B *Any seven points from the following:*

(i) 1. (translation) occurs on ribosomes
or mRNA attaches to /goes to/lines up on ribosomes
2. mRNA has groups of 3/triplets of bases/nucleotides called codons
3. each codon codes for a specific amino acid
or sequence of bases on mRNA determines sequence of amino acids in protein
4. tRNA molecules have groups of 3/triplets of bases/nucleotides called anti-codons
4a. **NB Only award if neither 2 nor 4 given**
mRNA has codons and tRNA has anticodons

5. tRNA molecules attach to/carry specific amino acids
6. tRNA molecules carry amino acids to mRNA/ribosomes
7. anti-codons link to / bond to / match with /line up against codons
   NOT triplets
8. complementary bases pair
   or A links to U and G links to C
9. amino acids are joined by peptide bonds

Any three points from the following:
(ii) 10. amino acid sequences/order determines protein shape/structure/function/type
11. (molecular) shape determines protein function
12. proteins can be fibrous or globular
13. fibrous eg collagen/structural component (of cells)
    or other named example such as keratin/actin/myosin
14. globular eg enzyme/antibody/hormone

2A *Any eight points from the following:*
(i) 1. blood water must be kept within limits/isotonic/at the same concentration as the tissues/at normal level/at a set point
2. (control involves) negative feedback
3. changes/decrease in blood water detected by hypothalamus **NOT** osmoreceptors alone
4. nerve messages/impulses sent to pituitary (gland)
5. pituitary increases the level of ADH released/produces more ADH
6. ADH transported to kidney via blood
7. ADH increases the permeability of kidney tubules to water
8. ADH allows more water to be reabsorbed **NOT** absorbed
9. water reabsorbed by osmosis
10. low/small volumes of concentrated urine produced
11. blood water returns to normal level/set point/norm
12. corrective mechanism switched off

2B *Any four points from the following:*
1. each (plant) community alters habitat/soil structure/soil depth/soil pH making it more suitable for next community/other species
2. succession is unidirectional
   or description of at least three communities in sequence with time indicated
3. species diversity/biodiversity increases
   or climax community has highest/higher species diversity/biodiversity
4. biomass increases
   or climax community has highest/higher biomass
5. food webs become more complex
   or climax community has more/most complex food webs
6. climax communities are the final/last communities produced
   or succession proceeds until/leads to the climax community

AND *any four points from the following:*
7. to provide (essential) data
8. ensure supply of/manage/set quotas for food/example of food species
   or stop overfishing
9. ensure supply of/manage raw materials/example of raw material species
10. control of/limit damage caused by pest species/pest population/pests
    or example of control of pests

11. pollution indicator/indicator species/biological indicator
12. protect/conserve endangered species
    or prevent extinction of endangered species